WILLIAMS-SONOMA

New American Cooking

# The Heartland

GENERAL EDITOR **Chuck Williams**

RECIPES AND TEXT **Beth Dooley**

FOOD PHOTOGRAPHY **Leigh Beisch**

TIME
LIFE
BOOKS

# New Ameri

The Pacific Northwest

California

The

The Southwest

# Table of **Contents**

# Introduction

When people ask me to describe Heartland food, the image I conjure is of Bettye Olson's hot dish, my first meal some twenty years ago in what was then my new hometown of Minneapolis.

That memorable one-pot supper wasn't the swampy green beans and canned fried onions that I had somehow been led to believe epitomized the Heartland menu. Rather, Bettye, my neighbor, created a fragrant dinner of nutty wild rice, sugar snap peas, spicy sausage, and bubbling cheese. "The peas are from my garden, and a friend, a potter, made the baking dish," she said.

Over the years, Bettye has taught me how to make two-fisted cinnamon buns and how to clean walleye for panfrying over an open fire. Together, we have filled coffee cans with raspberries, foraged for morel mushrooms after a spring rain, and wandered farmers' markets at dawn.

Today, the Heartland table is a mix of the old and the new. It celebrates both long-established culinary traditions and a rich mix of contemporary ethnic flavors. The region's cooks simmer hearty soups and stews for family dinners, bake towering chiffon cakes for church potlucks, assemble Asian curries from a pantry of exotic spices, and boast about their locally raised heirloom fruits and vegetables and organic meats and poultry. Simply put, Heartland cooking is good home cooking.

## A Vast and Diverse Region

The Heartland defies state boundaries. Whereas the Midwest is typically described as including Minnesota, Iowa, Wisconsin, Michigan, Illinois, Indiana, and Ohio, the Heartland is more expansive. Although it limits Ohio to its western portion, it adds northern Missouri, the eastern lowlands of Kansas, Nebraska, and North and South Dakota to the culinary map. This sizable swath embraces thick northern forests and the Great Lakes, rolling grasslands and open prairies, rich dark soil and the mighty Mississippi.

Home to many Native American tribes, including the Ojibway, Sioux, Menominee, Winnebago, Orapahoe, Omaha, Lakota, Iowa, Cherokee, and Missouri, the region was opened by explorers and trappers, settled by farmers, and developed by the mining, logging, fishing, and milling entrepreneurs who seeded its bustling urban centers.

A wealth of natural resources fed the railroad and steamship systems that carried the region's goods out to the world and brought in newcomers from distant shores. Each wave of immigrants—Scandinavians, Eastern Europeans, Welsh, Scots, Germans, Italians, Russians—contributed to the local larder, planting seeds from their homelands and sharing their skills as dairymen, butchers, bakers, and brewers. At Christmastime, the aromas of a kitchen identified its inhabitants: German aniseed, Norwegian cardamom, Russian caraway, and Hungarian paprika.

Iron ore mines in northern Minnesota, Wisconsin, and Michigan—

an area called the Iron Range—drew immigrants from Eastern Europe, Wales, and Italy. Their bold, hearty food now attracts campers who vacation in the dense woods and along the shores of Lakes Superior and Michigan. Travel down to Minneapolis, Chicago, and Detroit, and find Hmong sweet-and-sour soup, Indian curry, and Somalian peanut chicken joining the eclectic Heartland smorgasbord.

## Potlucks, State Fairs, and Bake-Offs

The term *neighboring* describes what happens when someone who lives nearby bangs through the screen door without knocking to borrow some sugar and stays to help finish off the morning coffee. The typical long distances between rural homes, the solitary nature of farm work, and the fierce extremes of the region's weather have contributed to a genuine delight in the company of others.

Not surprisingly, neighboring gave rise to the potluck, which finds cooks carrying dishes to share at family reunions, political gatherings, sports team banquets, and even weddings. Such occasions inevitably reflect the varied ethnic backgrounds of Heartland neighbors, with everything from pasties (Cornish meat pies) to sarma (Croatian cabbage rolls) on the menu at these homespun feasts.

Many Heartlanders like to show off their culinary and other wares at yet another of the region's traditional gatherings, the state fair. Minnesota, Iowa, Kansas, and Wisconsin are famous for these annual events, with each state competing to see who can draw the most people to the two-week extravaganzas. A legacy of early harvest festivals, the fairs showcase prize livestock, farm equipment, and blue-ribbon cakes, pies, pickles, jams and jellies, quilts, and seed art. Politicians strut their agendas and shake countless hands, while kids flock to midways to ride mammoth Ferris wheels and slowly rotating merry-go-rounds.

Homey and satisfying, this Turkey Noodle Soup (opposite and page 18) is delicious made with home-made egg noodles, a staple of the Amish kitchen. Red cabbage (above) is mixed with apples and cider vinegar for a sweet-sour combination in Braised Red Cabbage with Ginger (page 95).

11

Pickles and condiments of all kinds, such as Pickled Red and Gold Beets (above and page 92), continue to be favorite offerings of many Heartland cooks. Roast Duck with Sweet-and-Sour Sauce (right and page 66) is a delicious way to prepare the day's quarry. Sour Cream–Brown Sugar Cookies (opposite above and page 110) are a perfect ending to any Heartland meal.

But competition among Heartland cooks is not limited to vying for blue ribbons at state fairs. In the past, farm women would try to outdo one another with gargantuan meals to attract the best crews come threshing and barn-raising time. These days, cooks seek big prize money and fame through the Pillsbury Bake Off, the American Royal/K.C. Masterpiece International Invitational Barbecue Contest, and the Gedney Pickle Recipe Contest, to name just a few of the many high-stakes culinary events.

## From Corporate Giants to Weekend Anglers

A growing number of small-scale entrepreneurs and a healthy handful of multinational corporations are critical to the Heartland's vibrant food scene. Native Americans continue to hand-harvest wild rice with canoes and tap trees for maple syrup, and artisan producers make jams and jellies from wild fruits. Small flour mills use grinding stones to turn organic hard spring wheat into whole-wheat (whole-meal) flour, and microbreweries

make beer the traditional German way from corn, rye, wheat, and even wild rice.

Farmstead cheeses fashioned from the milk of cows, sheep, and goats rival many of those in Europe. Organic farmers who grow vegetables or raise pork, dairy cows, beef cattle, chickens, and turkeys have established the Coulee Region Organic Produce Pool (CROPP), the country's largest organic farmers' cooperative. Not far away is Land O'Lakes, the world's largest dairy cooperative. Among the familiar international corporate giants who boast Midwest headquarters are General Mills, Pillsbury, Kellogg, International Multifoods, Anheuser-Busch, and Archers Daniels Midland.

The region's anglers and hunters are also responsible for keeping kitchens well stocked. In the spring, the cold lakes and fast streams draw folks in search of feisty bass, trout, and walleye. In fall, the woods and fields are thick with hunters stalking deer, quail, woodcocks, and partridge. Winter tests the

hardiest to carve holes in the ice for fishing, with the most dedicated anglers raising huts and establishing ice villages with named streets on the largest lakes. In spring, foragers head out in search of morel mushrooms and know that ramps, or wild leeks, and watercress will follow.

The story of the Heartland table features family farmers and corporate titans, Native Americans and

new immigrants. In recent years, home cooks have developed a growing commitment to fresh, healthful, locally produced foods and a revitalized respect for the hearty comfort foods that have fueled residents for decades. Heartland cooking is best described as an unpretentious and generous fare—a table meant for sharing with family and friends.

# 1 Soups & One-Dish Meals

Soups, stews, and one-dish meals are the hallmarks of Midwestern cooking. Seasonal and satisfying, they are wonderfully flexible, doing double duty as first courses or main dishes and traveling smoothly to neighborhood potlucks. A corn chowder celebrates the golden light of August, whether as a tantalizing opener or a hearty feast in a pot. Come spring, a savory strudel captures the woodsy flavor of wild mushrooms in a flaky crust. A batch of Michigan pasties or a summer gratin makes a reliable meal, easy to prepare ahead of time for a large gathering or to welcome you home after a busy day.

# Turkey Noodle Soup

4 lb (2 kg) turkey parts

1 large yellow onion, chopped

2 carrots, chopped

1 celery stalk with leaves, chopped

5 fresh flat-leaf (Italian) parsley
  sprigs

3 fresh thyme sprigs

1 bay leaf

3 qt (3 l) water

salt to taste


6 oz (185 g) dried egg noodles

2 carrots, peeled and chopped

1 celery stalk with leaves, chopped

½ cup (1½ oz/45 g) chopped green
  cabbage

1 cup (6 oz/185 g) fresh or frozen
  corn kernels

2 tablespoons chopped fresh dill
  or 1 teaspoon dried dill

3 tablespoons chopped fresh flat-leaf
  (Italian) parsley

salt and freshly ground pepper to taste

The simmering soup pot that once warmed every Amish and Mennonite communal kitchen seems ideal for today's busy cooks. Simple and homey, the soup practically cooks itself.

1.  To make the stock, cut the turkey parts into smaller pieces to speed the cooking. Place the turkey, onion, carrots, celery, parsley, thyme, and bay leaf in a stockpot and pour in the water. Bring just to a boil, skimming any foam that rises to the surface. Cover partially and adjust the heat so that the stock barely bubbles. Simmer gently, continuing to skim as necessary, until the meat is opaque throughout, 45–55 minutes.

2.  Remove from the heat and pour through a sieve placed over a large bowl. Press on the vegetables and the meat with the back of a spoon to extract as much liquid as possible. Season the stock with the salt. Remove the meat from the bones, discarding the fat and bones along with the vegetables. Shred the meat and reserve for adding to the soup.

3.  Skim the fat from the stock. Pour off 2 qt (2 l) to use for the soup; reserve the remaining stock for another use.

4.  Bring a saucepan three-fourths full of salted water to a boil. Add the noodles and cook until al dente, 8–10 minutes. Drain and set aside.

5.  While the noodles are cooking, in a large soup pot over medium heat, combine the 2 qt (2 l) stock, the carrots, the celery, and the cabbage. Bring to a simmer and cook until the vegetables are tender, 5–8 minutes.

6.  Stir in the reserved shredded turkey, the drained noodles, the corn, the dill, and 2 tablespoons of the parsley. Season with salt and pepper. Simmer until heated through and the corn is tender, a few minutes.

7.  Ladle into warmed bowls and garnish with the remaining 1 tablespoon parsley. Serve at once.

SERVES 6-8

NUTRITIONAL ANALYSIS PER SERVING
Calories 264 (Kilojoules 1,109); Protein 25 g; Carbohydrates 28 g; Total Fat 6 g;
Saturated Fat 2 g; Cholesterol 71 mg; Sodium 192 mg; Dietary Fiber 2 g

# Summer Gratin with Olives

4 boiling potatoes, about 1 lb (500 g) total weight, peeled and cut into rounds ½ inch (12 mm) thick

½ cup (4 fl oz/125 ml) extra-virgin olive oil, plus extra if needed

salt and freshly ground pepper to taste

1 large eggplant (aubergine), or 2–3 Asian (slender) or small white eggplants (aubergines), about 1 lb (500 g) total weight, unpeeled, cut into rounds ½ inch (12 mm) thick

4 small zucchini (courgettes), about 1 lb (500 g) total weight, cut into rounds ½ inch (12 mm) thick

3 red (Spanish) onions, cut into rounds ½ inch (12 mm) thick

4 tomatoes, cut into rounds 1 inch (2.5 cm) thick

4 cloves garlic, crushed

1 cup (5 oz/155 g) mixed pitted olives such as Kalamata, green colossal, and herbed black

1 cup (4 oz/125 g) shredded Asiago cheese (optional)

Try the different kinds of eggplants available, such as small white and slender Asian varieties, in farmers' markets and roadside stands in this easy and forgiving dish. It almost can't be overbaked: the longer it cooks, the more the vegetables melt into one another. Leftovers are delicious stuffed in a pita sandwich or tossed with pasta.

1. Preheat the oven to 375°F (190°C).

2. Lay the potatoes over the bottom of an ovenproof 9-by-13-inch (23-by-33-cm) baking dish. Drizzle with 2 tablespoons of the olive oil and sprinkle with salt and pepper.

3. In a large bowl, stir together the eggplant, zucchini, onions, tomatoes, and the garlic with the remaining 6 tablespoons (3 fl oz/90 ml) oil and arrange them over the potatoes. Scatter the olives over the vegetables. Cover the baking dish tightly with aluminum foil.

4. Bake for 30 minutes. Remove the foil and continue baking until the vegetables are cooked through, 45–60 minutes. If the vegetables appear to be getting dry, brush with additional oil.

5. Remove from the oven and sprinkle with the cheese, if using. Serve hot or at room temperature.

SERVES 6 AS A MAIN COURSE, OR 8-10 AS A SIDE DISH

NUTRITIONAL ANALYSIS PER MAIN-COURSE SERVING
Calories 335 (Kilojo        )7); Protein 5 g; Carbohydrates 31 g; Total Fat 23 g; Saturated Fat 3 g; Cholesterol 0 mg; Sodium 464 mg; Dietary Fiber 5 g

# Sweet Corn Chowder

8–10 large ears of corn, husks and silk removed

4 slices thick-cut bacon, cut into ½-inch (12-mm) pieces

1 yellow onion, chopped

½ lb (250 g) red or white boiling potatoes, peeled and chopped

4 cups (32 fl oz/1 l) vegetable or chicken stock

1 bay leaf

2 tablespoons chopped fresh thyme or 2 teaspoons dried thyme

1½–2 cups (12–16 fl oz/375–500 ml) milk, or as needed

1 red bell pepper (capsicum), seeded and diced

1–3 tablespoons Canadian whiskey, to taste (optional)

generous pinch of red pepper flakes, or to taste

salt and freshly ground black pepper to taste

¼ cup (⅓ oz/10 g) chopped fresh flat-leaf (Italian) parsley

In late summer, the corn in Iowa is so sweet that the farmers at market give out samples cut right off the cob. Less than an hour out of the field, fresh corn hardly needs to be cooked. A splash of Canadian whiskey, made of distilled corn and other grains, gives this sweet, smooth chowder a nice rough edge. Simmer the cobs in the stock for extra flavor.

1. Working with 1 ear of corn at a time, hold it stem end down on a cutting board. Using a sharp knife, and starting from the top, carefully cut off the kernels, rotating the ear after each cut until all the kernels are stripped from the cob. Set the kernels and the cobs aside separately. You should have about 4 cups (1½ lb/750 g) corn kernels.

2. In a heavy soup pot over medium heat, fry the bacon until crisp, about 5 minutes. Using a slotted spoon, transfer the bacon to paper towels to drain. Add the onion to the bacon drippings in the pot and sauté over medium heat until translucent, about 10 minutes.

3. Add the potatoes, stock, bay leaf, thyme, 2 cups (12 oz/375 g) of the corn kernels, and the cobs. Simmer, uncovered, until the potatoes are tender, 12–15 minutes.

4. Remove the bay leaf and the cobs and discard. Working in batches, pour the mixture into a blender or food processor and purée until smooth. Return to the pot.

5. Set the pot over low heat and stir in the remaining corn kernels, enough of the milk to arrive at a nice consistency, the bell pepper, the whiskey (if using), and the red pepper flakes. Season with salt and black pepper. Ladle into warmed bowls and sprinkle with the bacon and the parsley.

**SERVES 6 AS A FIRST COURSE, OR 4 AS A MAIN COURSE**

NUTRITIONAL ANALYSIS PER FIRST-COURSE SERVING
Calories 324 (Kilojoules 1,436); Protein 9 g; Carbohydrates 34 g; Total Fat 19 g; Saturated Fat 7 g; Cholesterol 27 mg; Sodium 894 mg; Dietary Fiber 5 g

Come August in the Heartland, corn hangs on residents' minds like a summer haze. The annual rite of husking ears, loosening silk, and letting the juices run free is at hand, and nearly everyone participates.

Today's sweet corn varieties produce ears so sweet that seed catalogs classify them by sugar percentages: "Sweet" (5 to 10 percent sugar) bred for flavor and crispness, and "Sugar Enhanced" (15 to 18 percent) and "Supersweet" (25 to 30 percent sugar), which balance sweetness with juiciness. Popular varieties include Kandy Korn (sweet yellow), Bodacious (supersweet yellow), and Butter and Sugar (sweet bicolor), all types that are particularly good for canning.

Organic corn varieties include red, purple, and bicolored yellow and white and have more-complex flavors than their commercial counterparts. Most farmers hand-pick their organic corn to ensure that the ears are fully mature and to prevent the ears from getting bruised or damaged in the process, which often happens during machine-harvesting.

The best way to cook corn? Get the ears from the corn patch into

# Sweet **Corn**

a pot of boiling water as quickly as possible, watch for the color to darken (about a minute or so), and then take the corn out of the water right away. Never salt the water, as it toughens the kernels; and although cooks once put milk or sugar in the water to revive overly mature ears, the excellent corn available today makes such additions unnecessary.

# Mushroom and Onion Strudel

## STRUDEL

3 lb (1.5 kg) mixed fresh mushrooms such as oyster, shiitake, portobello, morel, and cremini, brushed clean or rinsed if laden with grit and cut into 1-inch (2.5-cm) pieces

2 sweet yellow or white onions, cut into 1-inch (2.5-cm) pieces

about ¼ cup (2 fl oz/60 ml) olive oil

2 teaspoons coarse salt

grated zest of 1 orange

juice of 1 orange

¼ cup (⅓ oz/10 g) chopped fresh flat-leaf (Italian) parsley

2 tablespoons chopped fresh rosemary

2 cloves garlic, coarsely chopped

1 teaspoon freshly ground pepper

8 sheets filo dough, thawed in the refrigerator if frozen

¼ cup (2 oz/60 g) unsalted butter, melted and cooled

## SAUCE

2 tablespoons olive oil

2 yellow onions, chopped

2 cloves garlic

4 red bell peppers (capiscums), seeded and sliced

1 red or green jalapeño chile, seeded and sliced (optional)

2 tablespoons tomato paste

1 tablespoon balsamic vinegar

salt and freshly ground pepper to taste

This savory vegetable strudel makes a stunning first course or simple dinner.

1. To make the strudel, preheat the oven to 400°F (200°C). In a large bowl, toss the mushrooms and onions with oil to coat generously. Sprinkle with the salt. Spread the vegetables, the pieces not touching, in roasting pans. Roast until the mushrooms are tender and begin to brown and the onions are golden, 20–30 minutes. Transfer to a bowl and toss in the orange zest and juice, parsley, rosemary, garlic, and pepper.

2. Reduce the heat to 350°F (180°C). Lightly butter a baking sheet or line with parchment (baking) paper. Lay 2 sheets of the filo dough on a large piece of waxed paper. (Cover the other sheets with a damp cloth to prevent drying.) Brush the top sheet with some butter, top with a single sheet, and brush it with butter. Continue adding sheets, brushing each one with butter, until all 8 sheets are used. Mound the filling lengthwise down the center of the filo, leaving 2 inches (5 cm) uncovered on all sides. Fold in a long side, overlapping the filling by 1 inch (2.5 cm). Fold in the short ends, then roll up to enclose the filling completely. Place seam side down on the prepared baking sheet. Brush the top and sides with the remaining butter. Bake until browned and crisp, about 40 minutes.

3. Meanwhile, make the sauce: In a frying pan over medium heat, warm the oil. Add the onions and garlic and sauté until translucent, about 3 minutes. Add the bell peppers and the chile, if using, and cook until very soft, 7–10 minutes. Purée in a blender until smooth, press through a sieve, stir in the tomato paste, vinegar, salt, and pepper, and reheat.

4. Let the strudel rest for 3 minutes, then cut on the diagonal into slices 3 inches (7.5 cm) thick. Serve with the warm sauce.

SERVES 6–8 AS A FIRST COURSE, OR 4–6 AS A MAIN COURSE

NUTRITIONAL ANALYSIS PER FIRST-COURSE SERVING
Calories 342 (Kilojoules 1,436); Protein 8 g; Carbohydrates 35 g; Total Fat 21 g; Saturated Fat 6 g; Cholesterol 18 mg; Sodium 579 mg; Dietary Fiber 5 g

# Fire and Ice Gazpacho

⅔ small loaf French or Italian bread, crusts removed and cubed (about 2 cups/4 oz/125 g)

2 or 3 Beefsteak or other large tomatoes, cut into chunks

1 cucumber, peeled, halved, seeded, and chopped

½ small red (Spanish) onion, chopped

1 clove garlic

1 red jalapeño chile, chopped (optional)

3–4 cups (24–32 fl oz/750 ml–1 l) tomato juice

2 tablespoons extra-virgin olive oil

2 tablespoons sherry vinegar

salt and freshly ground pepper to taste

½ cup (¾ oz/20 g) chopped fresh basil

2 cups (12 oz/375 g) mixed yellow and red cherry tomatoes

1 lemon, cut into wedges

CONDIMENTS

1 cucumber, peeled, halved, seeded, and finely diced

1 yellow or orange tomato, seeded and finely diced

½ red (Spanish) onion, finely diced

1 each red, green, and yellow bell pepper (capsicum), seeded and finely diced

3 hard-boiled eggs, peeled and finely diced

½ cup (¾ oz/20 g) chopped fresh basil

½ cup (¾ oz/20 g) chopped fresh cilantro (fresh coriander)

Spicy hot with chile, this refreshing, cold soup provides a delicious way to showcase summertime tomatoes.

1. In a blender, combine the bread cubes, tomatoes, cucumber, onion, garlic, chile (if using), 3 cups (24 fl oz/750 ml) tomato juice, oil, and vinegar. Purée until smooth, about 2 minutes. Add more tomato juice as needed for a good consistency. Pour into a bowl, cover, and refrigerate for at least 4 hours or up to overnight. Chill short glasses or soup bowls for serving.

2. Place each condiment in a separate small bowl. Remove the soup from the refrigerator. If it is too thick, thin it with a little ice water, then season with salt and pepper. Stir in the chopped basil and ladle into the chilled glasses or bowls. Remove the stems from the cherry tomatoes, quarter the tomatoes lengthwise, and scatter them on top of each serving. Serve with the lemon wedges. Pass the condiments at the table for your guests to add to their bowls as they like.

SERVES 4–6

NUTRITIONAL ANALYSIS PER SERVING
Calories 274 (Kilojoules 1,151); Protein 11 g; Carbohydrates 40 g; Total Fat 11 g; Saturated Fat 2 g; Cholesterol 128 mg; Sodium 822 mg; Dietary Fiber 7 g

# Spring Vegetable Stew with Hazelnuts

Spring fever hits Heartlanders hard. As the days lengthen and our appetites lighten, we yearn for quick, easy fare. Sunchokes, also known as Jerusalem artichokes and Canadian potatoes, grow wild across the Midwest and are a favorite of spring-time cooks. The plant grows up to ten feet (3 m) tall and produces yellow blossoms that turn their heads to follow the sun. Unlike potatoes, these tubers do not store well.

1. Preheat the oven to 400°F (200°C). Spread the nuts on a baking sheet and toast until the skins begin to darken and crack, about 10 minutes. Remove from the oven, wrap the still-warm nuts in a clean kitchen towel, and rub between your palms to remove the skins. Chop coarsely and set aside.

2. Bring a large pot three-fourths full of salted water to a boil. Add the pasta, stir well, and cook until al dente, 8–12 minutes or according to package directions.

3. Meanwhile, in a large frying pan over medium-low heat, melt the butter until foamy. Just as it begins to brown and smell nutty, toss in the asparagus, mushrooms, sunchokes, turnips, and carrot. Sauté, stirring often, for 1–2 minutes. Sprinkle the vegetables with the thyme and nutmeg and add the stock, wine, and cream. Bring to a boil over high heat and cook until reduced and thickened and the flavors have married and intensified, about 5 minutes.

4. Drain the pasta and transfer to a warmed serving dish. Stir the lemon juice, lemon zest, salt, and pepper into the vegetables and spoon over the pasta. Sprinkle with the hazelnuts and garnish with the lemon wedges. Serve immediately.

SERVES 4-6

NUTRITIONAL ANALYSIS PER SERVING
Calories 508 (Kilojoules 2,134); Protein 14 g; Carbohydrates 57 g; Total Fat 26 g; Saturated Fat 11 g; Cholesterol 51 mg; Sodium 314 mg; Dietary Fiber 7 g

½ cup (2½ oz/75 g) hazelnuts (filberts)

½ lb (250 g) radiatore or other dried spiral pasta

3 tablespoons unsalted butter

1 lb (500 g) asparagus, tough stems removed and cut into 1-inch (2.5-cm) pieces

1 lb (500 g) mixed fresh mushrooms such as cremini, portobello, morel, and shiitake, brushed clean or rinsed if laden with grit and cut into 1-inch (2.5-cm) pieces

½ lb (250 g) sunchokes, peeled and cut into 1-inch (2.5-cm) pieces

2 small turnips, peeled and cut into 1-inch (2.5-cm) pieces

1 carrot, peeled and cut into 1-inch (2.5-cm) pieces

2 teaspoons chopped fresh thyme or 1 teaspoon dried thyme

⅛ teaspoon freshly grated nutmeg

½ cup (4 fl oz/125 ml) chicken stock

½ cup (4 fl oz/125 ml) dry white wine

½ cup (4 fl oz/125 ml) heavy (double) cream

1 tablespoon fresh lemon juice

1 teaspoon grated lemon zest, or to taste

salt and freshly ground pepper to taste

1 lemon, cut into wedges

# Pasties with Garlic and Fresh Herbs

## PASTRY

3 cups (15 oz/470 g) all-purpose (plain) flour

1 teaspoon salt

½ cup (4 oz/125 g) chilled unsalted butter, cut into small pieces

2 egg yolks

6–8 tablespoons (3–4 fl oz/90–125 ml) ice water

## FILLING

½ lb (250 g) beef sirloin, finely diced

½ lb (250 g) pork butt, finely diced

1 carrot, peeled and diced

1 yellow onion, diced

1 turnip, peeled and diced

1 baking potato, peeled and diced

3 cloves garlic, minced

2 tablespoons chopped fresh flat-leaf (Italian) parsley

1 tablespoon chopped fresh marjoram or 2 teaspoons dried marjoram

1 tablespoon chopped fresh thyme or 2 teaspoons dried thyme

¼ teaspoon freshly grated nutmeg

generous pinch of red pepper flakes

1½ teaspoons salt

1 teaspoon freshly ground black pepper

4 tablespoons (2 oz/60 g) unsalted butter

chili sauce or ketchup

Two-fisted savory meat turnovers, pasties (pronounced pass-tees) are the pride of home cooks along the Iron Range. Minnesotans serve them with ketchup, while Michiganders favor chili sauce. Plan on 2 pasties each for large appetites and 1 each for medium-sized ones.

1. To make the pastry, in a food processor, combine the flour and salt and pulse to mix. Add the butter and pulse until the dough is crumbly. Add the egg yolks and 6 tablespoons (3 fl oz/90 ml) of the water and pulse just until the dough begins to come together, adding the remaining water if the mixture is too dry. Turn it out onto a work surface, gather into a ball, wrap in plastic wrap, and refrigerate for at least 1 hour or overnight.

2. Meanwhile, make the filling: In a bowl, toss together the beef, pork, carrot, onion, turnip, potato, garlic, parsley, marjoram, thyme, nutmeg, red pepper flakes, salt, and black pepper.

3. Preheat the oven to 375°F (190°C). Lightly butter a baking sheet or line with parchment (baking) paper.

4. On a floured work surface, divide the dough into 4 equal pieces. Roll out each piece into a disk ½ inch (12 mm) thick, then cut into a 5-inch (13-cm) round. Place one-fourth of the meat mixture on one-half of each round, leaving a ½-inch (12-mm) border, and top each with 1 tablespoon of the butter. Moisten the edges of the round with water. Fold the other half of the round over the meat, creating a half-moon, and seal the edges with fork tines. Cut 2 or 3 diagonal slashes into the top of each pasty. Place them on the prepared baking sheet.

5. Bake until the crusts are firm and brown, 50–60 minutes. Cover loosely with aluminum foil if the pasties begin to overbrown after 35 minutes of baking. Serve hot with chili sauce or ketchup.

MAKES 4 PASTIES; SERVES 2–4

NUTRITIONAL ANALYSIS PER PASTY
Calories 1,068 (Kilojoules 4,486); Protein 36 g; Carbohydrates 101 g; Total Fat 57 g; Saturated Fat 29 g; Cholesterol 278 mg; Sodium 1,568 mg; Dietary Fiber 6 g

# Yellow Pea Soup with Caraway

2 cups (14 oz/440 g) dried yellow peas

1 tablespoon unsalted butter

1 small yellow onion, chopped

2 small inner celery stalks with leaves, chopped

1 carrot, peeled and chopped

1 teaspoon caraway seeds

2 teaspoons grated orange zest

1 bay leaf

½ teaspoon ground turmeric

¼ cup (2 fl oz/60 ml) dry sherry (optional)

1 small ham bone or ham hock (optional)

4 cups (32 fl oz/1 l) vegetable or chicken stock

salt and freshly ground pepper to taste

Yellow pea soup, warming fare for a cold winter's night, remains a favorite traditional supper among Swedish families who settled the farmland and northern tier of Minnesota, Wisconsin, and Iowa. Caraway and orange zest give the golden, silky soup a pleasant tang.

1. Pick over the peas, removing any stones or misshapen peas. Rinse thoroughly and set aside.

2. In a heavy soup pot over medium heat, melt the butter. Add the onion, celery, and carrot and sauté until the onion is translucent, about 10 minutes. Add the peas, caraway seeds, orange zest, bay leaf, turmeric, and the sherry and ham bone or hock, if using. Pour in the stock, raise the heat to medium-high, and bring to a gentle boil. Cover, reduce the heat to medium-low, and cook until the peas are tender, 45–60 minutes. Remove from the heat and lift out the ham bone or hock, if used. When cool enough to handle, cut off and dice the meat and reserve.

3. In a blender or food processor, purée the soup, in batches, until the soup is smoother but still retains some texture. Season with salt and pepper. Return the soup to the pot and add the meat, if used. Heat to serving temperature.

4. Ladle into warmed soup bowls and serve at once.

SERVES 4–6

NUTRITIONAL ANALYSIS PER SERVING
Calories 328 (Kilojoules 1,378); Protein 20 g; Carbohydrates 55 g; Total Fat 4 g; Saturated Fat 2 g; Cholesterol 6 mg; Sodium 832 mg; Dietary Fiber 6 g

# Beef Stew with Stout

This is a rich stew, made with dark, creamy stout and infused with orange and rosemary. Start it early in the day or, better, a day ahead, to allow time for all the flavors to marry. It's delicious served on a bed of barley or Horseradish Mashed Potatoes (page 102).

1. Preheat the oven to 300°F (150°C). In a heavy ovenproof pot over medium-high heat, warm 1 tablespoon of the olive oil. When the oil is hot, add the meat cubes to the pot and sear on all sides, 6–8 minutes. Using a slotted spoon, transfer to a plate and set aside.

2. In the same pot over medium-low heat, warm the remaining 2 tablespoons olive oil. Add the onion, carrots, and garlic and sauté until the onion begins to darken, about 5 minutes. Sprinkle with the flour and cook, stirring, until it turns golden brown, about 3 minutes longer. Stir in the tomato paste and then return the meat to the pot. Slowly pour in the stout, stirring and allowing the liquid to thicken. Gather together the bay leaves, rosemary, thyme, parsley, and orange peel and tie with kitchen string to form a bouquet garni. Slip it into the liquid and bring to a boil. Season with salt and pepper, cover, and place in the oven. Bake until the meat is very tender, about 2 hours.

3. Remove the bouquet garni and discard. Ladle the stew into warmed individual bowls and serve at once.

SERVES 6–8

NUTRITIONAL ANALYSIS PER SERVING
Calories 411 (Kilojoules 1,726); Protein 39 g; Carbohydrates 16 g; Total Fat 20 g;
Saturated Fat 6 g; Cholesterol 126 mg; Sodium 195 mg; Dietary Fiber 3 g

3 tablespoons olive oil

3 lb (1.5 kg) boneless chuck steak, trimmed of excess fat and cut into 2-inch (5-cm) cubes

1 large yellow onion, chopped

1 lb (500 g) carrots, peeled and cut into 1-inch (2.5-cm) pieces

6 cloves garlic, peeled but left whole

2 tablespoons all-purpose (plain) flour

1 tablespoon tomato paste

3 cups (24 fl oz/750 ml) stout or dark beer

3 bay leaves

2 fresh rosemary sprigs

2 fresh thyme sprigs

2 fresh flat-leaf (Italian) parsley sprigs

3 strips orange peel

salt and freshly ground pepper to taste

# Whitefish Chowder

### GARLIC TOASTS

2 cloves garlic

3 tablespoons extra-virgin olive oil

1 baguette, cut into slices 1 inch
   (2.5 cm) thick

2 tablespoons vegetable oil

1 large yellow onion, finely chopped

2 small inner celery stalks with leaves,
   chopped

2 cloves garlic

2 tablespoons chopped fresh flat-leaf
   (Italian) parsley

1 tablespoon chopped fresh thyme

3 tablespoons tomato paste

1 lb (500 g) red or white boiling
   potatoes, peeled and cut into
   ½-inch (12-mm) dice

4 large, ripe tomatoes, peeled and
   cut into ½-inch (12-mm) dice,
   or 2 cups (12 oz/375 g) canned
   tomatoes, drained and chopped

4 cups (32 fl oz/1 l) vegetable stock

½ cup (4 fl oz/125 ml) dry white wine

1 bay leaf

½ teaspoon red pepper flakes,
   or to taste

grated zest of 1 orange

2 lb (1 kg) whitefish fillets, cut into
   2-inch (5-cm) chunks

salt and freshly ground black pepper
   to taste

¼ cup (⅓ oz/10 g) chopped fresh
   basil

Loaded with plump tomatoes and fresh herbs, this hearty chowder conjures up fall afternoons of long shadows and of red-tipped maple trees in the hills near Lake Superior. Whitefish, a firm, dense relative of the salmon, swims in Midwest streams and deep lakes. Cod or salmon may be substituted.

1. To make the garlic toasts, preheat the oven to 350°F (180°C). In a small bowl, crush the garlic with the back of a fork and add the olive oil. Brush the bread slices with the garlic oil on one side and place, oiled side up, on a baking sheet. Toast until the edges are brown and the bread is crusty, 5–10 minutes. Remove from the oven and set aside.

2. In a heavy soup pot over medium heat, warm the vegetable oil. Add the onion, celery, garlic, parsley, and thyme and sauté until the onion is translucent, about 10 minutes.

3. Stir in the tomato paste and add the potatoes, tomatoes, stock, wine, bay leaf, red pepper flakes, and zest. Bring to a simmer and cook, uncovered, until the potatoes are almost tender, 10–15 minutes.

4. Measure out about 1 cup (8 fl oz/250 ml) and pour into a blender or food processor. Purée until smooth and return the purée to the pot.

5. Bring the chowder to a boil, then reduce the heat so that the liquid simmers gently. Add the fish, cover the pan, and simmer until the fish is just done, 10–15 minutes. Discard the bay leaf. Season with salt and black pepper and stir in the basil.

6. Ladle into warmed bowls and float a garlic toast on top of each serving. Place the remaining toasts in a basket at the table.

SERVES 4–6

NUTRITIONAL ANALYSIS PER SERVING
Calories 641 (Kilojoules 2,692); Protein 43 g; Carbohydrates 57 g; Total Fat 27 g; Saturated Fat 4 g; Cholesterol 109 mg; Sodium 1,284 mg; Dietary Fiber 6 g

From late spring to early winter, anglers and hunters—locals and visitors alike—are drawn to the bounty of regional wildlife. The deep, cold lakes and swift streams of the Heartland hold the promise of a trophy trout, walleye, or bass, while the region's forests house pheasants, ducks, grouse, woodcocks, quail, rabbits, and venison.

The fishing season begins each year on The Opener, the second weekend in May. New licenses in hand, fishermen head to the northern lakes for two days of mostly male camaraderie.

Along the northern shore of Wisconsin's Lake Superior, fish boils, casual outdoor feasts, signal summer's arrival. Potatoes, onions, and whitefish are boiled in a huge pot of heavily salted water set over a wood fire. Just before the vegetables and fish are done, kerosene is thrown onto the fire, causing the pot to boil over and the impurities to run off. The fish is served with melted butter and, traditionally, rolls or rye bread, coleslaw, and fresh fruit crisp.

In autumn, when the shadows lengthen and the air turns crisp, hunters descend on the prairies and woods. Some seek a weekend's solitude in hunting shacks tucked into

# Fishing and **Hunting**

the forest, while others prefer predawn, preworkday jaunts into the open fields. Many families take this opportunity to fill their freezers with game and game birds. Fortunately, nonhunters can purchase farm-raised game at grocery stores and meat markets in the region, although a nonmigratory lifestyle results in flesh that lacks the distinctive taste of the wild.

# Hunter's Cassoulet

2¼ cups (1 lb/500 g) dried navy beans

1 yellow onion, chopped

2 carrots, peeled and chopped

2 celery stalks with leaves, chopped

4 cloves garlic, crushed

4 fresh thyme sprigs or 1 teaspoon
  dried thyme

1 bay leaf

¼ lb (125 g) slab bacon or salt pork,
  in one piece

1 lb (500 g) sweet Italian sausage,
  cut into 2-inch (5-cm) chunks

1 lb (500 g) boneless pork shoulder
  or butt, trimmed of excess fat,
  cut into 2-inch (5-cm) chunks

1 lb (500 g) boneless shoulder or leg
  of lamb, trimmed of excess fat, cut
  into 2-inch (5-cm) chunks

1 cup (8 fl oz/250 ml) dry red wine

2 cups (12 oz/375 g) canned plum
  (Roma) tomatoes, chopped

2 tablespoons tomato paste

3 tablespoons chopped fresh flat-leaf
  (Italian) parsley

1 tablespoon chopped fresh thyme

2 cloves garlic, chopped

salt and freshly ground pepper to taste

TOPPING

1 cup (4 oz/125 g) toasted bread
  crumbs

1 cup (1½ oz/45 g) finely minced
  fresh parsley

This recipe is a shortcut version of the classic French meat-and-bean dish, as warming today as it was for the early French trappers and voyageurs who made new lives in the Heartland.

1. Pick over the beans and discard any stones or misshapen beans. Rinse well, place in a large bowl, and add water to cover. Let soak overnight.

2. Drain the beans and place in a Dutch oven or other large, heavy pot. Add the onion, carrots, celery, garlic, thyme, bay leaf, and water to cover by about ½ inch (12 mm). Bring to a boil over high heat, skimming off any foam on the surface. Reduce the heat to low, cover partially, and simmer, stirring occasionally, until the beans are tender but still hold their shape, 20–25 minutes. Drain, then return the beans to the Dutch oven or pot, reserving half of the cooking liquid.

3. Meanwhile, in a small saucepan, combine the bacon or salt pork with water to cover. Bring to a boil and cook for about 2 minutes. Drain, dice the meat, and add to the beans. Preheat the oven to 375°F (190°C).

4. In a large frying pan over medium-high heat, cook first the sausage, then the pork and the lamb, in batches, until browned on all sides, about 15 minutes for each batch. Drain off and discard the fat after browning each batch and add each batch of browned meat to the beans as it is finished.

5. When the last batch is removed, pour in the wine and deglaze the pan, scraping up all the browned bits on the bottom. Stir in the tomatoes and tomato paste and simmer until reduced slightly, about 3 minutes. Add to the beans. Stir in the parsley, thyme, garlic, salt, and pepper. Pour in enough of the reserved bean liquid just to cover the beans and stir well.

6. To make the topping, combine the bread crumbs with ¾ cup (1 oz/30 g) of the parsley. Spread it over the beans and place in the oven. Bake until the beans are very tender and the topping is browned, about 45 minutes. Garnish with the remaining ¼ cup (½ oz/15 g) parsley and serve.

SERVES 8-10

NUTRITIONAL ANALYSIS PER SERVING
Calories 592 (Kilojoules 2,486); Protein 42 g; Carbohydrates 48 g; Total Fat 26 g;
Saturated Fat 9 g; Cholesterol 104 mg; Sodium 724 mg; Dietary Fiber 7 g

# Minted Double Pea Soup

2 tablespoons unsalted butter

2 small inner celery stalks with leaves, chopped

1 yellow onion, chopped

6 cups (48 fl oz/1.5 l) chicken stock

1 baking potato, peeled and sliced

2 fresh thyme sprigs

⅛ teaspoon freshly grated nutmeg

2 lb (1 kg) sugar snap peas, chopped

2 lb (1 kg) English peas, shelled, or 2 cups (10 oz/315 g) frozen shelled English peas, thawed

¼ cup (¼ oz/7 g) fresh flat-leaf (Italian) parsley leaves

¼ cup (2 fl oz/60 ml) heavy (double) cream, or to taste

2 tablespoons fresh lemon juice

salt and freshly ground pepper to taste

2 tablespoons chopped fresh mint, plus 4–6 sprigs

The sugar snap, darling of pea lovers, is a cross of the snow pea (mangetout) and the English pea and is sweeter and more succulent than its forebears. At the farmers' markets in Minneapolis and St. Paul, Hmong farmers (refugees from northern Laos) sell sugar snaps on the vine by the case. If you can find them this way, remove the pea pods and steep the vines for a few moments in the stock before making the soup, to add more luscious, rich, sweet pea flavor.

1. In a heavy soup pot over medium heat, melt the butter. Add the celery and onion and sauté until the onion is translucent and the celery is soft, about 5 minutes. Add the stock, potato, thyme, and nutmeg and bring to a boil. Reduce the heat to medium-low, partially cover the pot, and simmer until the potato slices are very tender, about 10 minutes.

2. Add the sugar snap peas and simmer until tender, 10–15 minutes. Add the English peas and simmer until cooked, 3–5 minutes. Stir in the parsley.

3. In a blender or food processor, purée the soup, in batches, until smooth. Pour through a sieve placed over a bowl resting in a bowl of ice. Stir the soup slowly until it has cooled to room temperature (this sets the green color). Stir in the cream, lemon juice, salt, and pepper, then remove the soup from the ice bath.

4. If serving the soup warm, return to the pot over low heat and heat through; do not allow it to boil. Or, if serving the soup cold, cover the bowl and refrigerate until well chilled.

5. Just before serving, taste and adjust the seasoning, stir in the chopped mint, and ladle into bowls or cups. Garnish with the mint sprigs and serve.

SERVES 4–6

NUTRITIONAL ANALYSIS PER SERVING
Calories 285 (Kilojoules 1,197); Protein 11 g; Carbohydrates 33 g; Total Fat 12 g; Saturated Fat 6 g; Cholesterol 29 mg; Sodium 1,223 mg; Dietary Fiber 8 g

# Sour Cherry–Riesling Soup

2 cups (16 fl oz/500 ml) dry Riesling

2 cups (16 fl oz/500 ml) cherry juice

2¼ lb (1.1 kg) fresh sour cherries, pitted, or 2 lb (1 kg) pitted frozen sour cherries

½ cup (3 oz/90 g) dried sour cherries

1 cinnamon stick, about 2 inches (5 cm) long

¼ cup (3 oz/90 g) honey

¼ cup (2 fl oz/60 ml) fresh orange juice

2 tablespoons cornstarch (cornflour)

1 tablespoon grated orange zest

½ cup (4 oz/125 g) sour cream or plain yogurt

¼ teaspoon ground cardamom

This lovely German-inspired soup makes a light, pretty first course on a hot summer evening. If sour cherries are unavailable, use fresh or frozen Bing cherries and dried cranberries and reduce the amount of honey to 1 tablespoon, or to taste. Serve this luscious pink soup for dessert, if you like, and garnish with sweetened, whipped heavy (double) cream.

1. In a wide soup pot over medium heat, combine the wine, cherry juice, half of the fresh or frozen cherries, the dried cherries, and the cinnamon stick. Bring to a simmer, reduce the heat to low, and cook, uncovered, until the cherries are soft, about 15 minutes. Remove from the heat and remove the cinnamon stick and discard.

2. In a blender or food processor, purée the soup, in batches, until the cherries are finely chopped but retain their texture. Return to the pot.

3. In a small bowl, stir together the honey, orange juice, cornstarch, and orange zest to make a paste. Whisk the paste into the soup and place over low heat. Cook, stirring occasionally, until thickened, about 5 minutes. Stir in the remaining cherries. Transfer the soup to a bowl, cover, and refrigerate to chill thoroughly, about 1½ hours. Chill the bowls or mugs in which you plan to serve the soup.

4. In a small bowl, stir together the sour cream or yogurt and cardamom. Ladle the soup into the chilled bowls or mugs and top each serving with a dollop of the cardamom-spiced cream. Serve at once.

**SERVES 6**

NUTRITIONAL ANALYSIS PER SERVING
Calories 310 (Kilojoules 1,302); Protein 2 g; Carbohydrates 57 g; Total Fat 4 g; Saturated Fat 3 g; Cholesterol 8 mg; Sodium 25 mg; Dietary Fiber 0 g

One magical week each May, the four million cherry trees surrounding Traverse City, Michigan, burst into bloom. Pure white blossoms hang above the gentle hills, with Lake Michigan's azure waters as a backdrop. First planted by Presbyterian missionary Peter Dougherty in the mid–nineteenth century, the trees thrive in the area's well-drained sandy soil and the unusually moderate climate created by the large lake. Michigan is the nation's leader in sour cherry production, and from early July through August, the world's largest sour cherry harvest takes place there.

Sour cherries such as English Morello and Montmorency, the most popular variety, are smaller, softer, and rounder than such sweet varieties as Bing and Emperor Frances. Too tart to eat raw, they add an appealing tang to preserves and pies, hence their other names, pie or tart cherries. To substitute sour cherries in recipes calling for sweet cherries, increase the amount of sugar by half or more to taste. They are delicate and perishable, so use them immediately.

Sour cherries are sold fresh for a few weeks, then the balance is

# Sour **Cherries**

canned, frozen, or dried. Wonderful mixed into muffin and cake batters, they also make a good substitute for the blueberries in the Deep-Dish Apple-Blueberry Pie on page 116, although you will need to increase the amount of sugar to temper the cherries' natural tartness. Dried sour cherries can replace raisins or chopped dried apricots in most recipes.

# 2 Poultry, Fish, Meat & Game

Be it a hefty Iowa pork chop, delicate walleye, or crispy roast duck, the main course is taken seriously by many Midwesterners. The region boasts a bounty of freshwater fish from cold lakes and wild game from big woods, and a sprawling patchwork of farms delivers free-range poultry, hogs, and cattle to local butcher shops. The German traditions of smoking meats and making sausage are very much alive today. Grilling over an open campfire or over a backyard grill is preferred by those who love to be outdoors. Indeed, Midwesterners will even shovel through a snowbank to throw a flank steak over a bed of hot coals or to tend a slow-cooking Kansas City BBQ.

# Farmhouse Roast Chicken with Pan Gravy

CHICKEN

1 roasting chicken, 3–5 lb (1.5–2.5 kg)

3 tablespoons unsalted butter,
   at room temperature

½ teaspoon coarse salt

¼ teaspoon freshly ground pepper

2 fresh tarragon sprigs

5 fresh flat-leaf (Italian) parsley sprigs

GRAVY

2 tablespoons all-purpose (plain) flour

3 cups (24 fl oz/750 ml) chicken stock

2 tablespoons chopped fresh flat-leaf
   (Italian) parsley

1 tablespoon chopped fresh tarragon

2 tablespoons brandy (optional)

salt and freshly ground pepper to taste

You don't have to live on a farm in the Midwest, and it doesn't have to be Sunday, to enjoy this old-fashioned chicken that in the past was the typical centerpiece of the big midday family meal following church services.

1. Preheat the oven to 450°F (230°C). Remove the giblets from the chicken's cavity and reserve for another use. Rinse the chicken inside and out and pat dry with paper towels. Rub the outside of the chicken with butter, then gently loosen the skin and slide some butter under it to coat evenly. Sprinkle the outside and the cavity with the salt and pepper, and place the tarragon and parsley in the cavity. Tie the legs together for a nicer presentation, if you like. Put the chicken, breast side up, on a V-shaped rack set in a roasting pan just larger than the rack.

2. Roast for 15–20 minutes. Reduce the heat to 375°F (190°C) and continue roasting until an instant-read thermometer inserted into the thickest part of the thigh away from the bone registers 170°F (71°C) or the juices run clear when the thigh is pierced with a fork, about 45 minutes for a 3-lb (1.5-kg) chicken. For larger birds, add 10 minutes for each additional pound (500 g). Transfer the chicken to a warmed platter and tent with aluminum foil to keep warm. Remove the rack from the pan.

3. To make the gravy, pour the pan juices into a saucepan and skim off the fat, reserving about 2 tablespoons. Spoon the 2 tablespoons fat back into the roasting pan, sprinkle the bottom of the pan with the flour, set on the stove top over low heat, and scrape the pan bottom to loosen the bits of dark drippings. Cook over low heat, stirring constantly, until smooth, about 5 minutes. Gradually stir in the pan juices, stock, parsley, and tarragon. Cook, stirring occasionally, until the mixture thickens, about 5 minutes. Add the brandy, if using, and season with salt and pepper.

4. Carve the chicken and arrange on the platter. Pour the gravy into a warmed bowl and pass at the table.

**SERVES 4–6**

NUTRITIONAL ANALYSIS PER SERVING
Calories 555 (Kilojoules 2,331); Protein 47 g; Carbohydrates 3 g; Total Fat 38 g;
Saturated Fat 13 g; Cholesterol 165 mg; Sodium 885 mg; Dietary Fiber 0 g

# Sage-Grilled Trout

4 trout, about 1 lb (500 g) each, cleaned

8 large fresh sage sprigs, plus extra sprigs for garnish

lemon slices (optional)

SAGE BUTTER

½ cup (4 oz/125 g) unsalted butter

⅓ cup (3 fl oz/80 ml) fresh lemon juice

2 tablespoons minced fresh sage

½ teaspoon coarsely ground pepper

salt to taste

Whole trout are well suited to the grill. The skin keeps the flesh moist and tender, and those who don't care for it can easily peel it off, although they are sacrificing a great deal of flavor. When making this recipe, grill an extra trout or two. Cold grilled trout has a slight smoky flavor that makes a wonderful salad with mixed young lettuces and a light vinaigrette.

1. Prepare a fire in a grill.

2. Rinse the trout inside and out under cold running water and pat them dry with paper towels. Place the trout in a shallow baking dish, then insert 2 sage sprigs in the cavity of each trout.

3. To make the sage butter, in a small pan over low heat, melt the butter and stir in the lemon juice, sage, pepper, and salt. Pour half of this mixture into a small bowl and set aside. Brush the remaining butter over the inside and outside of each trout.

4. Place the trout on the grill rack and cook until the skin begins to tighten over the flesh, about 4 minutes. Flip and cook until the fish are crisp and well browned, about 4 minutes longer.

5. Transfer the trout to a warmed platter, brush with some of the reserved sage butter, and garnish with the sage sprigs and lemon slices, if you like. Pass the remaining sage butter at the table.

**SERVES 4**

NUTRITIONAL ANALYSIS PER SERVING
Calories 540 (Kilojoules 2,268); Protein 47 g; Carbohydrates 2 g; Total Fat 38 g; Saturated Fat 17 g; Cholesterol 191 mg; Sodium 119 mg; Dietary Fiber 0 g

# Pork Chops with Sage Applesauce

APPLESAUCE

2 cups (16 fl oz/500 ml) fresh apple
cider

4 large, tart apples such as Haralson,
McIntosh, or Cortland, peeled,
halved, cored, and cut into 1-inch
(2.5-cm) chunks

2 tablespoons chopped fresh sage
or 1 teaspoon dried sage

pinch of sugar, or to taste

pinch of freshly grated nutmeg,
or to taste

1 tablespoon freshly ground black
pepper

pinch of cayenne pepper

1 teaspoon Dijon mustard

3 tablespoons olive oil

4 premium loin pork chops, each
about 10 oz (315 g) and 1½ inches
(4 cm) thick

4 small fresh sage sprigs

The Iowa pork chop is not just any pork chop. It is a very thick, lean center-cut loin or rib chop that weighs in at about 10 ounces (315 g). In this recipe, a dry seasoning rub penetrates the meat with extra flavor. The sage applesauce is also great with roast turkey or Farmhouse Roast Chicken with Pan Gravy (page 42).

1. To make the applesauce, combine the cider and apples in a heavy saucepan and place over high heat. Bring to a boil, reduce the heat to medium-low, cover, and simmer, stirring occasionally, until the apples have softened completely and begin to break apart, 20–30 minutes. The applesauce should be thick and chunky; if there is too much liquid, remove the lid and simmer, uncovered, until thickened. Stir in the sage and cook for another 5 minutes to blend the flavors, then add the sugar and nutmeg.

2. Preheat the oven to 400°F (200°C).

3. To prepare the pork chops, mix together the black pepper, cayenne pepper, and mustard with 1 tablespoon of the olive oil. Rub the chops with the spice mix. (You may do this up to 1 day ahead, cover the chops tightly with plastic wrap, and store in the refrigerator. The longer they stand, the more flavor they will have.)

4. In a frying pan over high heat, warm the remaining 2 tablespoons oil. Add the chops and sear, turning once, until golden brown, 3–4 minutes on each side. Transfer the chops to a baking sheet and bake until the juices run a rosy color, 15–20 minutes.

5. Transfer the chops to warmed individual plates, and accompany each chop with a dollop of warm applesauce alongside. Garnish with the sage sprigs. Pass the remaining applesauce at the table.

SERVES 4

NUTRITIONAL ANALYSIS PER SERVING
Calories 799 (Kilojoules 3,356); Protein 57 g; Carbohydrates 54 g; Total Fat 40 g;
Saturated Fat 12 g; Cholesterol 170 mg; Sodium 168 mg; Dietary Fiber 5 g

I n Iowa, hogs outnumber people. Iowa remains the biggest pork producer in the world. Indeed, pork is king here, and each year at the state fair, a panel of judges crowns a lissome young woman Pork Queen, a much-sought-after local honor.

Despite the hog's continuing high status, Iowa's hog farmers have witnessed dramatic changes in recent times. Over the last decade, almost half of the state's pork producers went out of business. Their demise is linked to the corporate takeover of the bulk of Iowa's pork production, a fact that has rocked the economy and affected the flavor and quality of the meat.

Modern hogs are bred to minimize fat, thus satisfying consumer demand for a healthier diet. But fat is what gives pork much of its flavor and what helps to keep it from drying out during cooking.

Happily, a new crop of producers is raising hogs the old-fashioned way, giving them lots of room to roam— free-range—and shunning the use of growth hormones in their feed. They are relying on breeds of animals that can withstand the cold weather because of their generous layers of fat. The hogs yield firmer, almost buttery

# Iowa **Pork**

meat with a bright, fresh taste.

Free-range pork is more expensive than conventionally raised pork, of course, but it is well worth it. Small producers sell their meat through local cooperatives, and savvy Iowa consumers know that if they pay the extra cost, they will be rewarded with superior meat—pork that deserves its royal status.

# Walleye in Parchment with Lemon and Dill

6 tablespoons (3 oz/90 g) unsalted
butter, at room temperature

4 walleye fillets, 4–6 oz (125–185 g)
each

1 lemon, thinly sliced

4–8 fresh dill sprigs

4–8 fresh flat-leaf (Italian) parsley
sprigs

8 dashes of Tabasco or other hot-
pepper sauce

salt and freshly ground pepper to taste

Walleye, often called the sole of freshwater fish, is snowy white, fine flaked, sweet, and tender. Although sometimes called walleye pike, the fish is not a pike at all, but instead a member of the perch family and closely related to the sweet yellow perch. On the Wolf River in Wisconsin, walleyes migrate a hundred miles upstream from Lake Winnebago, to the delight of northern Heartland sport fishers. If walleye is not available, substitute sole, snapper, or flounder in this recipe.

1. Preheat the oven to 350°F (180°C). Cut four 24-by-12-inch (60-by-30-cm) pieces of parchment (baking) paper. Using 2 tablespoons of the butter, liberally butter each sheet.

2. Rinse the fillets and pat dry with paper towels. Place 1 walleye fillet at one wide end of the parchment, leaving about 2 inches (5 cm) of paper uncovered at the bottom. Put 2 or 3 slices of lemon, 1 or 2 dill sprigs, and 1 or 2 parsley sprigs on top of each fillet. Shake 2 dashes of hot-pepper sauce over each fillet. Season the fish with salt and pepper. Dot each fillet with equal amounts of the remaining 4 tablespoons (2 oz/60 g) butter.

3. To close the parchment paper, moisten the edges of the paper with water. Fold the free half of the paper over the fish, closing it like a book. Fold the edges of the paper over, crimping as you go, to enclose the fish. Assemble the remaining 3 packets, and place all the packets on a baking sheet.

4. Bake until the parchment paper is puffed and brown, 10–12 minutes.

5. Place the packets on individual plates, slit open carefully, avoiding the steam, and fold back the parchment. Serve at once.

SERVES 4

NUTRITIONAL ANALYSIS PER SERVING
Calories 215 (Kilojoules 903); Protein 28 g; Carbohydrates 3 g; Total Fat 10 g;
Saturated Fat 6 g; Cholesterol 145 mg; Sodium 80 mg; Dietary Fiber 1 g

# Kansas City–Style BBQ

DRY RUB

⅓ cup (3 oz/90 g) firmly packed brown sugar

¼ cup (1¼ oz/37 g) sweet paprika

3 tablespoons freshly ground pepper

2 tablespoons chile powder

1 tablespoon coarse salt

1 beef brisket, 5 lb (2.5 kg), trimmed of excess fat

SAUCE

1 tablespoon vegetable oil

1 small yellow onion, chopped

3 cloves garlic, minced

1½ cups (12 fl oz/375 ml) ketchup

2 tablespoons brown sugar

2 tablespoons Worcestershire sauce

2 teaspoons prepared horseradish

2 teaspoons cider vinegar

1 bay leaf

1 teaspoon chile powder

1 teaspoon freshly ground pepper

2 or 3 drops Tabasco or other hot-pepper sauce

During the Depression, Henry Perry, the father of Kansas City–style barbecue, prepared great slabs of beef in an outdoor pit, sold them in sandwiches wrapped in newspaper, and made the city—and its barbecue—world famous.

1. To make the dry rub, in a small bowl, stir together the brown sugar, paprika, pepper, chile powder, and salt. Rub the brisket all over with the dry rub. Cover with plastic wrap and refrigerate overnight.

2. Prepare an indirect-heat fire in a covered grill. When the coals are white with ash, place chunks of hickory or fruit wood (apple or cherry) on top. (If using a gas grill, preheat to low, then place the wood on top.)

3. Place the meat, fat side up, on the center of the grill rack, cover, and barely open the vents. Cook the meat for 10 minutes, then turn and cook for another 10 minutes to seal the outside of the meat. Turn again, replace the lid, and continue to cook the meat at about 225°F (110°C), turning two or three times, until an instant-read thermometer inserted into the thickest part registers 165°F (74°C) or until tender, about 3 hours.

4. Remove the meat from the grill, wrap tightly in aluminum foil, return to the grill, and continue cooking at about 200°F (95°C) until the meat is very tender, 2–3 hours longer. Remove the meat from the grill and let rest in the foil for about 10 minutes.

5. To make the sauce, in a saucepan over low heat, warm the vegetable oil. Add the onion and sauté until translucent, 7–8 minutes, then add the garlic and sauté until the garlic softens, 2–3 minutes longer. Add the ketchup, brown sugar, Worcestershire sauce, horseradish, vinegar, bay leaf, chile powder, pepper, and hot-pepper sauce and simmer, uncovered, until slightly thickened, 7–10 minutes.

6. Thinly slice the meat and arrange on a warmed platter. Pour the sauce into a warmed bowl and pass at the table.

SERVES 8–12

NUTRITIONAL ANALYSIS PER SERVING
Calories 403 (Kilojoules 1,693); Protein 36 g; Carbohydrates 27 g; Total Fat 17 g; Saturated Fat 6 g; Cholesterol 108 mg; Sodium 1,008 mg; Dietary Fiber 2 g

# Lamb Chops with Rosemary-Mint Sauce

1 clove garlic, crushed

1 yellow onion, chopped

1 teaspoon ground cumin

½ teaspoon sweet paprika

2 tablespoons red wine vinegar

2 tablespoons olive oil

8 rib or loin lamb chops

SAUCE

8 cups (8 oz/250 g) fresh mint leaves,
    plus sprigs for garnish (optional)

2 tablespoons chopped fresh rosemary

2 tablespoons sugar

¼ cup (2 fl oz/60 ml) champagne
    vinegar

This snappy mint sauce is inspired by a recipe from one of the Heartland's first cookbooks, *Buckeye Cookery and Practical Housekeeping,* published in Ohio and Minnesota in the early 1800s. The recipe offers a delicious, practical, and timeless solution for too much backyard fresh mint.

1. In a blender or food processor, combine the garlic, onion, cumin, paprika, vinegar, and olive oil and process until smooth. Spread the paste over the lamb chops, cover with plastic wrap, and marinate at room temperature for 1 hour or in the refrigerator for up to overnight.

2. To make the sauce, in a food processor, combine the mint leaves, rosemary, and sugar and process until finely chopped but not puréed. Transfer to a small bowl and stir in the vinegar. Cover and refrigerate until serving. (The sauce will keep for up to 1 week.)

3. Preheat the broiler (griller).

4. Scrape the marinade from the chops. Place the chops on a broiler pan and broil (grill), turning once, until nicely browned on both sides and still pink in the center, 2–3 minutes on each side, or until done to your liking.

5. Transfer the lamb chops to warmed individual plates, garnish with mint sprigs, if you like, and pass the sauce at the table.

SERVES 4

NUTRITIONAL ANALYSIS PER SERVING
Calories 645 (Kilojoules 2,709); Protein 34 g; Carbohydrates 16 g; Total Fat 49 g; Saturated Fat 19 g; Cholesterol 140 mg; Sodium 127 mg; Dietary Fiber 5 g

# Grilled Coho Salmon with Cucumber Relish

CUCUMBER RELISH

3 small English (hothouse) cucumbers, peeled and diced

1 jalapeño chile, seeded and finely chopped

3 tablespoons finely chopped fresh flat-leaf (Italian) parsley leaves

3 tablespoons finely chopped fresh mint leaves

3 tablespoons extra-virgin olive oil

3 tablespoons fresh lemon juice, or to taste

pinch of sugar

salt and freshly ground pepper to taste

4 coho salmon, about ¾ lb (375 g) each, cleaned

12 fresh flat-leaf (Italian) parsley sprigs

olive oil for coating

4 fresh mint sprigs

Midwest coho salmon is farm-raised in cold, clear stream-fed ponds. Its flesh is firm and sweet like that of trout but with the light pink color of salmon. Serve the cohos with this refreshing, spicy cucumber-mint relish.

1. To make the relish, in a bowl, stir together the cucumbers, chile, parsley, mint, olive oil, lemon juice, and sugar. Season with salt and pepper. Set aside while you cook the salmon.

2. Prepare a fire in a grill.

3. Rinse the salmon inside and out under cold running water and pat them dry with paper towels. Place 3 parsley sprigs in the cavity of each salmon. Place the fish in a shallow nonaluminum pan and coat them all over with olive oil.

4. Place the salmon on the grill rack and cook until the skin begins to tighten over the flesh, about 4 minutes. Flip and cook until the flesh is opaque throughout, 3–4 minutes longer.

5. Transfer the salmon to warmed individual plates. Garnish each fish with a mint sprig and 1 or 2 spoonfuls of relish. Pass the remaining relish at the table.

SERVES 4

NUTRITIONAL ANALYSIS PER SERVING
Calories 471 (Kilojoules 1,978); Protein 50 g; Carbohydrates 6 g; Total Fat 27 g; Saturated Fat 5 g; Cholesterol 100 mg; Sodium 106 mg; Dietary Fiber 3 g

# Flank Steak with Gin-Juniper Marinade

½ cup (4 fl oz/125 ml) olive oil

3 tablespoons red wine vinegar

2 tablespoons gin

2 teaspoons chopped fresh thyme

2½ teaspoons juniper berries, crushed

½ teaspoon coarse salt, plus salt
to taste

½ teaspoon freshly ground pepper,
plus pepper to taste

1 flank steak, 1½ lb (750 g)

Heartland cattle farmers and butchers often sell their prime cuts and use interesting marinades and spice rubs to enjoy the tougher but more flavorful cuts. This simple marinade of juniper berries and thyme complements the rich taste of flank steak. Serve with Cracked Wheat Salad with Asparagus (page 104).

1. In a small bowl, whisk together the olive oil, vinegar, gin, thyme, juniper berries, and ½ teaspoon each salt and pepper. Put the steak into a nonaluminum pan, pour the marinade over it, and rub the marinade into the meat. Cover with plastic wrap and let stand at room temperature for 2 hours or refrigerate for up to overnight.

2. Preheat the broiler (griller). Remove the steak from the marinade, reserving the marinade, and season lightly with salt and pepper. In a small saucepan over high heat, bring the marinade to a boil. Broil (grill) the steak, basting occasionally with the marinade and turning once, until rare to medium-rare, 4–5 minutes on each side.

3. Transfer the steak to a cutting board and let rest for 5 minutes. Slice against the grain and arrange on a warmed platter. Serve at once.

SERVES 4

NUTRITIONAL ANALYSIS PER SERVING
Calories 403 (Kilojoules 1,693); Protein 33 g; Carbohydrates 0 g; Total Fat 29 g;
Saturated Fat 8 g; Cholesterol 85 mg; Sodium 192 mg; Dietary Fiber 0 g

# Grilled Venison with Maple-Mustard Glaze

1 clove garlic, crushed

2 tablespoons Dijon mustard

2 tablespoons vegetable oil

1 venison loin or 2 pork tenderloins,
   1¾–2 lb (750 g–1 kg)

4 slices thick-cut, lean, hickory-smoked
   bacon or Canadian bacon

¼ cup (2 fl oz/60 ml) maple syrup

The venison loin, sometimes called the backstrap, is a long, slender muscle tucked against the backbone. The fat in the bacon bastes the meat, but it can also cause flare-ups during grilling. Cook the loin over low, indirect heat and keep it moving, rolling from side to side. Pork tenderloin is easily substituted for venison in this recipe by simply adjusting the cooking time as noted below.

1. In a small bowl, stir together the garlic, mustard, and oil. Rub the mixture generously into the meat, cover tightly, and marinate in the refrigerator for 5–6 hours or for up to overnight.

2. Soak 4 toothpicks in water for 15 minutes. Wrap the bacon around the loin(s), covering completely, and secure with the soaked toothpicks.

3. Prepare an indirect-heat fire in a charcoal grill. Place the meat on the grill rack so that it is not directly over the coals and grill, rolling the loin(s) from side to side about every 5 minutes to prevent sticking or burning. About 5 minutes before the meat is ready, begin basting occasionally with the maple syrup. Cook until an instant-read thermometer inserted into the thickest part of the loin registers 136°F (58°C) for venison and 148°F (64°C) for pork or until the meat is crusty brown and the juices run a rosy color when the meat is pierced, 20–25 minutes for venison and 18–25 minutes for pork.

4. Transfer the loin(s) to a warmed platter, remove the toothpicks, and let the meat rest for 5–10 minutes. Slice into medallions and serve at once.

SERVES 4

NUTRITIONAL ANALYSIS PER SERVING
Calories 397 (Kilojoules 1,667); Protein 50 g; Carbohydrates 10 g; Total Fat 15 g;
Saturated Fat 4 g; Cholesterol 183 mg; Sodium 389 mg; Dietary Fiber 0 g

# Paprika Cornish Hens

Eastern European flavors remain prevalent in the northern mining towns of Michigan, Minnesota, and Wisconsin. Hungarian paprika gives a subtle sweet heat and complex taste to even the most straightforward dish. Serve these plump hens with wide egg noodles or wild rice.

1. Preheat the broiler (griller). Rinse the hens and pat dry. Using poultry shears, cut the backbones out of the hens. Split each hen in half lengthwise by cutting down one side of the breast.

2. In a small saucepan over low heat, combine the orange juice and raisins and heat for 1–2 minutes, then set aside to plump.

3. In a small bowl, stir together 1 teaspoon of the paprika, 1 teaspoon of the cinnamon, the nutmeg, ½ teaspoon salt, ¼ teaspoon pepper, and 2 tablespoons of the sour cream. Rub each hen half with an equal amount of the spice mixture. Place the hen halves skin side up on a broiler pan. Place the pan in the broiler 6 inches (15 cm) from the heat source and broil (grill), turning frequently, until the juices run clear when the thickest part of the thigh is pierced, 25–35 minutes.

4. About 15 minutes before the hens are ready, melt the butter in a saucepan over medium heat. Add the onion and sauté until translucent and very soft, about 8 minutes. Add the remaining 1 teaspoon each paprika and cinnamon and cook, stirring, for 1 minute. Add the stock and 1 cup (6 oz/185 g) of the raisins and their liquid and cook until the sauce is reduced by half and thickened, 3–4 minutes. Remove from the heat and swirl in the remaining sour cream. Add the vinegar and season with salt and pepper.

5. Arrange the birds on a warmed platter and cover with the sauce. Garnish with the remaining ¼ cup (2 oz/60 g) raisins and the parsley and serve.

SERVES 4–6

NUTRITIONAL ANALYSIS PER SERVING
Calories 651 (Kilojoules 2,734); Protein 37 g; Carbohydrates 46 g; Total Fat 36 g; Saturated Fat 13 g; Cholesterol 219 mg; Sodium 496 mg; Dietary Fiber 3 g

4 Cornish hens, about 1 lb (500 g) each

¾ cup (6 fl oz/180 ml) fresh orange juice

1¼ cups (8 oz/245 g) raisins

2 teaspoons sweet Hungarian paprika

2 teaspoons ground cinnamon

½ teaspoon freshly grated nutmeg

½ teaspoon salt, plus salt to taste

¼ teaspoon freshly ground pepper, plus pepper to taste

⅓ cup (3 oz/90 g) sour cream

2 tablespoons unsalted butter

1 large yellow onion, finely chopped

¾ cup (6 fl oz/180 ml) chicken stock

1–2 teaspoons red wine vinegar, or to taste

2 tablespoons chopped fresh flat-leaf (Italian) parsley, plus sprigs for garnish

# Braised Chicken with Rosemary and Tomatoes

3 lb (1.5 kg) chicken leg-and-thigh pieces

salt and freshly ground pepper to taste

2 tablespoons unsalted butter

1 red (Spanish) onion, thinly sliced

2 cloves garlic, sliced

½ cup (4 fl oz/125 ml) dry white wine

2 cups (12 oz/375 g) canned plum (Roma) tomatoes, chopped, with their juice

3 fresh rosemary sprigs or 1 teaspoon dried rosemary

3 fresh flat-leaf (Italian) parsley sprigs

While many of the nation's largest poultry producers are located in Minnesota, Wisconsin, and Iowa, a growing number of small family farms in these same three states raise free-range chickens and turkeys. Free-range chickens have big meaty thighs and slightly smaller breasts than conventional commercial chickens. This recipe cooks thighs and legs in a fruity tomato sauce over low heat until the meat is meltingly tender.

1. Rinse the chicken pieces and pat dry with paper towels. Sprinkle with salt and pepper.

2. In a frying pan large enough to accommodate all of the chicken pieces in a single layer, melt the butter over medium-high heat. Add the onion and sauté, turning the slices occasionally, until translucent, about 3 minutes.

3. Add the garlic and the chicken, skin side down. Cook until the skin forms a golden crust, about 5 minutes. Turn the pieces and cook the other side until the skin forms a golden crust, about 5 minutes. Using tongs, transfer to a plate and set aside.

4. Add the wine and deglaze the pan, scraping up all the browned bits on the bottom. Simmer until reduced by half, about 5 minutes. Add the tomatoes, rosemary, and parsley, reduce the heat to medium-low, and return the chicken to the pan. Cover partially and simmer, turning the chicken occasionally, until the chicken feels tender when prodded with a fork and the meat easily comes off the bone, 45–50 minutes.

5. Transfer to a warmed platter and serve immediately.

SERVES 4–6

NUTRITIONAL ANALYSIS PER SERVING
Calories 444 (Kilojoules 1,865); Protein 37 g; Carbohydrates 7 g; Total Fat 29 g; Saturated Fat 10 g; Cholesterol 177 mg; Sodium 274 mg; Dietary Fiber 1 g

# Blue Plate Meat Loaf

½ cup (1 oz/30 g) fresh bread crumbs

½ cup (4 fl oz/125 ml) buttermilk

1 lb (500 g) ground (minced) beef

½ lb (250 g) bulk pork sausage meat

½ lb (250 g) ground (minced) turkey
or veal

1 egg, lightly beaten

1 small yellow onion, minced

¼ cup (⅓ oz/10 g) minced fresh
flat-leaf (Italian) fresh parsley

½ teaspoon freshly ground pepper

¼ teaspoon salt

3 slices hickory-smoked bacon
(optional)

Thick slices of meat loaf, a pillow of mashed potatoes smothered with rich, dark gravy, and Perfect Green Beans (page 86) is a blue-plate special to tempt the traveler off any winding "blue highway." While opinions on meat loaf run deep, the best loaves are moist and honestly seasoned. No fussy ingredients like smoked peppers or capers, please. This loaf is shaped on the baking sheet (not pressed into a loaf pan), so that all three sides brown and the fat runs off the meat instead of being trapped in by the pan.

1. Preheat the oven to 350°F (180°C).

2. In a small bowl, soak the bread crumbs in the buttermilk until it is absorbed, about 3 minutes.

3. In a bowl, combine the soaked bread crumbs, beef, sausage, turkey or veal, egg, onion, and parsley. Gently mix together with your hands. Add the pepper and salt and mix again.

4. Turn the mixture onto a rimmed baking sheet and shape it into a loaf about 9 by 3 inches (23 by 7.5 cm). If using the bacon, lay the strips across the loaf lengthwise.

5. Bake, basting occasionally with the pan juices, until the meat loaf is lightly browned and firm and an instant-read thermometer inserted into its center registers 160°F (71°C), 45–55 minutes.

6. Using a serrated knife, cut the loaf into slices 1½ inches (4 cm) thick. Transfer to individual plates and serve.

SERVES 4-6

NUTRITIONAL ANALYSIS PER SERVING
Calories 487 (Kilojoules 2,045); Protein 31 g; Carbohydrates 7 g; Total Fat 37 g;
Saturated Fat 14 g; Cholesterol 162 mg; Sodium 560 mg; Dietary Fiber 1 g

# T-Bone Steak with Spicy Rub

1 tablespoon finely chopped fresh
   rosemary

2 tablespoons black peppercorns

2 tablespoons green peppercorns

pinch of cayenne pepper

2 teaspoons coarse salt

2 tablespoons extra-virgin olive oil

2 or 3 T-bone or porterhouse steaks,
   each about 2 lb (1 kg) and 1½ inches
   (4 cm) thick

The T-bone, like the porterhouse steak, is cut from the thicker part of the short loin and contains a portion of the top loin. Named for the bone that spreads in the shape of the letter across the top of the cut and tails through the center, the T-bone is a rich, well-marbled steak. Grill sun-ripened tomato halves or skewers of whole cherry tomatoes to serve alongside.

1. In a spice mill or using a mortar and pestle, combine the rosemary, black peppercorns, green peppercorns, and cayenne pepper. Grind finely and pour into a small bowl. Stir in the salt. Mix in the olive oil to make a paste.

2. Trim the fat from the steaks, leaving a layer ¼ inch (6 mm) thick. Rub the steaks with the spice mixture and place in a baking dish. Cover with plastic wrap and marinate at room temperature for 30 minutes.

3. Prepare a fire in a covered charcoal grill.

4. Place the steaks on the grill rack and sear on each side for 2 minutes. Cover the grill and cook, turning once, until the steaks are done to your liking, 3–4 minutes on each side for rare to medium-rare.

5. Transfer the steaks to a warmed platter and let rest for about 5 minutes before serving. Divide into 4 equal portions and serve at once.

SERVES 4

NUTRITIONAL ANALYSIS PER SERVING
Calories 699 (Kilojoules 2,936); Protein 87 g; Carbohydrates 2 g; Total Fat 36 g;
Saturated Fat 13 g; Cholesterol 247 mg; Sodium 1,092 mg; Dietary Fiber 1 g

A growing number of today's Midwest cattle farmers are quick to boast about their happy and healthy herds. Their stocky, sturdy, mostly Black Angus cattle, at home on the rolling hills of southern Wisconsin, Iowa, Minnesota, and Illinois, graze freely on sweet clover and feast on organic grains. They are never crowded into feedlots or fed food laced with the hormones and antibiotics that stimulate growth. The result is beef with an intensity of flavor that the factory-farmed competition could never match.

Many of the area's cattle farmers are members of the Coulee Region Organic Produce Pool (CROPP), a cooperative based in La Farge, Wisconsin, that markets its beef under the Organic Valley Farms label. Today, CROPP, which was begun in 1988 by seven local farmers, is the largest organic farmers' cooperative in North America.

Members are careful to protect waterways from pollutants and are dedicated to recycling nutrients back into the same soil that is planted with the grasses and grains used for feed. The cooperative relies on small, local processors, so that the cattle are not moved over long distances.

# Organic **Beef**

Because the federal government has not yet established standards for organic beef, consumers are advised to look for "negative" claims on packaging. Phrases such as "raised without hormones or antibiotics" and "raised on feed grown without pesticides or rendered animal products" are guarantees of the highest-quality Midwest beef.

# Roast Duck with Sweet-and-Sour Sauce

2 large ducks such as Pekin, 4–5 lb
(2–2.5 kg) each

coarse salt and freshly ground pepper
to taste

1 large shallot, chopped

½ cup (4 fl oz/125 ml) fresh apple
cider

¼ cup (2 fl oz/60 ml) cider vinegar

¼ cup (3 oz/90 g) honey, or to taste

2 tablespoons heavy (double) cream

1 teaspoon Dijon mustard

1 large, tart red apple such as Prairie
Spy, Cortland, or McIntosh, peeled,
halved, cored, and thinly sliced

regular salt to taste

Wild ducks are popular among Midwest cooks, but in this recipe, farm-raised ducks are on the menu. To keep them moist and crisp, prick the skin while they roast, so that their rendered fat will baste the ducks as they cook.

1. Preheat the oven to 500°F (260°C). Remove any giblets from the cavities and reserve for another use. Trim off the wing tips and any neck fat. Rinse the birds and pat dry with paper towels, then rub inside and out with coarse salt and pepper. Lightly prick the skin all over with a fork, being careful not to pierce the flesh. Put the ducks on a large rack in a large roasting pan.

2. Roast for 20 minutes. Reduce the heat to 365°F (185°C) and prick the ducks lightly again. Roast until the skin is golden brown and an instant-read thermometer inserted into the thickest part of the thigh away from the bone registers 170°F (75°C) or until juices are rosy to yellow, 55–65 minutes longer, depending on the size of the ducks. Transfer the ducks to a carving board and let rest for 15–30 minutes before carving.

3. While the ducks are resting, make the sauce: Pour off all but 2 table-spoons of the duck fat from the roasting pan and place the pan on the stove top over medium heat. Add the shallot and sauté until translucent, 2–3 minutes. Raise the heat to high, add the cider and vinegar, and deglaze the pan, scraping up any browned bits on the bottom. Cook until the liquid is reduced by half, 3–5 minutes. Reduce the heat to low and whisk in the ¼ cup (3 oz/90 g) honey, the cream, and the mustard. Add the apple slices and simmer until they are tender and the sauce is slightly thickened, about 5 minutes. Taste and adjust with a little honey, if needed. Season with salt and pepper.

4. Carve each duck into thigh-leg and boneless breast portions and arrange on a warmed serving platter. Drizzle with some of the sauce and pass the remaining sauce in a warmed bowl at the table.

SERVES 4–6

NUTRITIONAL ANALYSIS PER SERVING
Calories 337 (Kilojoules 1,415); Protein 23 g; Carbohydrates 23 g; Total Fat 17 g;
Saturated Fat 6 g; Cholesterol 126 mg; Sodium 113 mg; Dietary Fiber 1 g

# Roast Pork Loin with Garlic and Fennel

1 boneless pork loin, 2½ lb (1.25 kg)

6 cloves garlic, sliced

salt and freshly ground pepper to taste

2 tablespoons fennel seeds

6 fresh rosemary sprigs

6 fresh sage sprigs

6 fresh flat-leaf (Italian) parsley sprigs, plus chopped parsley for garnish

2 fennel bulbs, trimmed and quartered lengthwise

Some say the key to cooking today's lean pork so that it turns out moist and flavorful is to cook it quickly using high heat. Here, the loin is seasoned with garlic and fennel and then roasted for just an hour. The roast will be moist and barely pink when you're ready to carve and serve it.

1. A day in advance of serving, using a small, sharp knife, make incisions about 1 inch (2.5 cm) deep on the outside of the roast and insert the garlic slices. Season the roast with salt and pepper. Crush the fennel seeds in a mortar with a pestle and press over the meat. Press the rosemary, sage, and parsley sprigs into the meat. Roll up the roast and, using kitchen string, tie at regular intervals to maintain an even, compact shape. (If the roast comes with netting, remove the netting, prepare the roast as described above, and then replace the netting to cover and secure the seasonings and herbs.) Wrap the roast in plastic wrap and refrigerate for at least 4 hours or for up to overnight.

2. Preheat the oven to 425°F (220°C). Bring the roast to room temperature.

3. Set the roast on a rack in a roasting pan and put the quartered fennel bulbs in the bottom of the pan. Roast the pork loin until an instant-read thermometer inserted into the thickest part of the loin registers 140°F (60°C) or the center is slightly pink when cut into with a sharp knife, about 1 hour.

4. Remove the roast from the oven, cover loosely with aluminum foil, and let rest for 15 minutes. Snip the kitchen string and discard. Slice the pork and arrange on a warmed platter with the fennel quarters. Sprinkle with the chopped parsley and serve at once.

SERVES 4–6

NUTRITIONAL ANALYSIS PER SERVING
Calories 485 (Kilojoules 2,037); Protein 47 g; Carbohydrates 6 g; Total Fat 29 g; Saturated Fat 10 g; Cholesterol 143 mg; Sodium 239 mg; Dietary Fiber 2 g

# Beer Brats with Sauerkraut

6 bratwursts

1 red (Spanish) onion, cut into rings
   1 inch (2.5 cm) thick

2–2½ cups (16–20 fl oz/500–625 ml)
   German-style beer

2 cups (1 lb/500 g) sauerkraut

1 tablespoon caraway seeds

1 tart apple, unpeeled, halved, cored,
   and cut into 2-inch (5-cm) chunks

6 crusty long rolls, split horizontally

*Sauerkraut,* German for "sour cabbage," is the perfect foil for peppery bratwurst braised in beer. Fresh sauerkraut, sold in delicatessens and the refrigerated section of super-markets, comes closest to the tangy flavor of homemade "kraut" cured in big wooden barrels. German communities throughout the Midwest hold Oktoberfest celebrations with street fairs where vendors sell grilled bratwurst and sauer-kraut on crusty buns.

1. Prepare a fire in a grill, or preheat the broiler (griller).

2. Put the sausages and onion into a wide, deep pan and add beer as needed to cover them halfway. Bring the beer to a gentle boil and cook the sausages for about 10 minutes. Prick the sausages all over with a fork.

3. Place the sausages on the grill rack or on a broiler pan. Grill or broil, turning as needed, until nicely browned on all sides, 3–5 minutes.

4. Meanwhile, in a small saucepan over medium heat, combine the sauerkraut, caraway seeds, and apple. Bring to a gentle boil and cook until the apple is soft, about 5 minutes.

5. Place a sausage on each roll bottom, top with a spoonful of the sauerkraut, and close the rolls. Pass the remaining sauerkraut at the table.

SERVES 4–6

NUTRITIONAL ANALYSIS PER SERVING
Calories 703 (Kilojoules 2,953); Protein 29 g; Carbohydrates 58 g; Total Fat 39 g; Saturated Fat 13 g; Cholesterol 82 mg; Sodium 1,823 mg; Dietary Fiber 5 g

August Schell Brewery, founded in New Ulm, Minnesota, in 1860, is the granddaddy of the Midwest microbrewery movement. Best known for Schell Bock and Oktoberfest, rich malty-sweet brews for harvest celebrations, August Schell seeded a crop of independent breweries that continue to make beer the old-fashioned way.

Introduced by German immigrants, beer drinking was once a daily ritual in much of the region, and the *biergarten* was a place to relax, sing, and play musical instruments. Milwaukee's Pabst, Miller, Schlitz, and Blatz; St. Paul's Hamms; LaCrosse's Heilman; and St. Louis's Anheuser-Busch all got their start by supplying draft kegs to these gathering places. Joseph Schlitz Brewing Company produced the first bottled beer, which quickly "Made Milwaukee Famous."

In the early 1900s, Anheuser-Busch operated its own railroad to export its beer. In 1920, Prohibition put the brakes on industry expansion, and most breweries barely survived until 1933, when the law was repealed.

Since then, mass-produced American beer has become blander, lighter, and more uniform, as the number of breweries in the country

# Midwest **Microbrews**

has dropped from some two thousand to less than fifty. Upstart microbrews, in contrast, are distinguished by their deep color and robust flavors. Among the region's notable breweries are St. Paul's Summit; Rapid City, South Dakota's Firehouse; Lawrence, Kansas's Free State; Amana, Iowa's Millstream; and Chippewa Falls, Wisconsin's Leinenkugel's.

RAMPS $1.50 ea
WILD LEEKS
3 bunches /$4.00

GRADE
MILK

TURN
at the
CHURN

• BULLS
for SALE

WISCONSIN STATE BRAND
1710 WI D
OCT 17 1995
067

WISCONSIN STATE BRAND
1710 WI D
OCT 17 1995
067

# 3 Vegetables, Beans & Grains

In the Midwest, the land is fertile, the crops are plentiful, and the growing season is heartbreakingly short. Appetites follow the arc of the sun from spring's peppery watercress to July's plump tomatoes to August's golden corn to the sturdy beets, squashes, parsnips, and potatoes of autumn. Here you will find new takes on old favorites: gingery red cabbage, fresh soybean succotash, spaetzle with fresh herbs. Dishes of wild rice and cracked wheat make substantial sides or light centerpieces, and condiments fashioned from freshly harvested vegetables brighten a casual dinner or make thoughtful gifts. Try pairing recipes in this chapter for a satisfying vegetarian meal.

# Maple-Glazed Roasted Root Vegetables

2 carrots, scrubbed and cut into
2-inch (5-cm) pieces

1 large parsnip, scrubbed and cut
into 2-inch (5-cm) pieces

1 small turnip, scrubbed and cut into
2-inch (5-cm) pieces

½ rutabaga, scrubbed and cut into
2-inch (5-cm) pieces

1 sweet potato, peeled and cut into
2-inch (5-cm) pieces

1 red (Spanish) onion, cut into 2-inch
(5-cm) pieces

2–3 tablespoons vegetable oil

2 teaspoons coarse salt

¼ cup (2½ fl oz/75 ml) maple syrup

2 tablespoons unsalted butter, melted

This old-fashioned vegetable combination offers the best of a Heartland root cellar. Sweet potatoes in the Midwest have a drier flesh and are less sweet than those that grow down South. Turnips, sometimes called Swedish potatoes, and the ubiquitous rutabaga give a nice bitter edge to the bright carrots and sweet red onions. Try these alongside Pork Chops with Sage Applesauce (page 46).

1. Preheat the oven to 400°F (200°C).

2. In a large bowl, toss together the carrots, parsnip, turnip, rutabaga, sweet potato, and onion with enough vegetable oil to coat. Sprinkle with the salt and toss again. Spread the vegetables in a single layer without touching on baking sheets.

3. Roast, shaking the baking sheets occasionally and turning the vegetables with a spatula to keep them from sticking, until they develop a light crust and are tender, 40–50 minutes.

4. In a small bowl, stir together the maple syrup and butter. Brush over the vegetables and continue roasting until the vegetables look glazed, about 5 minutes longer.

5. Arrange the vegetables in a warmed serving dish and serve at once.

SERVES 4–6

NUTRITIONAL ANALYSIS PER SERVING
Calories 241 (Kilojoules 1,012); Protein 2 g; Carbohydrates 33 g; Total Fat 12 g;
Saturated Fat 4 g; Cholesterol 12 mg; Sodium 638 mg; Dietary Fiber 5 g

# Spaetzle with Thyme–Brown Butter

2 cups (10 oz/315 g) all-purpose (plain) flour

2 eggs

½ cup (4 fl oz/125 ml) heavy (double) cream

¼ cup (2 fl oz/60 ml) milk

2 tablespoons finely chopped fresh flat-leaf (Italian) parsley

1½ teaspoons finely chopped fresh thyme

¼ teaspoon salt

¼ teaspoon freshly ground pepper

⅛ teaspoon freshly grated nutmeg

½ cup (4 oz/125 g) unsalted butter

The word *spaetzle* means "little sparrow" in German, describing these tiny dumplings, traditionally served with roast meat and gravy. They are also delicious tossed with butter and herbs and dusted with a little grated cheese. While skilled cooks work the sticky dough between their fingers into a pot of boiling water, it is simpler to press it through a potato ricer or a colander, because the dough becomes easier to manipulate as it warms over the boiling liquid.

1. In a bowl, stir together the flour, eggs, cream, milk, 1 tablespoon of the parsley, 1 teaspoon of the thyme, salt, pepper, and nutmeg. Beat until the dough is smooth and elastic.

2. Fill a large pot three-fourths full of water and bring to a boil. Reduce the heat to a steady simmer.

3. Scoop out about ¼ cup (2 oz/60 g) of the dough and press it through a colander or ricer directly into the simmering water. Simmer until the dough pieces remain floating on the surface, about 2 minutes. Lift out with a slotted spoon, draining well, put into a serving dish, cover, and place in a low oven to keep warm. Repeat with the remaining dough. The spaetzle may be kept warm in a low oven for 10–15 minutes before serving.

4. In a small saucepan over medium-low heat, melt the butter with the remaining ½ teaspoon thyme. Cook, shaking the pan occasionally, just until the butter turns from yellow to medium brown, about 7 minutes. (Be careful. If cooked too long, the butter may burn, but if not cooked long enough, it will lack the nutty flavor characteristic of brown butter.)

5. Drizzle the spaetzle with the thyme–brown butter, sprinkle with the remaining 1 tablespoon parsley, and toss to mix. Transfer to a warmed serving bowl and serve immediately.

SERVES 4–6

NUTRITIONAL ANALYSIS PER SERVING
Calories 490 (Kilojoules 2,058); Protein 9 g; Carbohydrates 45 g; Total Fat 30 g; Saturated Fat 18 g; Cholesterol 169 mg; Sodium 159 mg; Dietary Fiber 2 g

# Autumn Apple Coleslaw with Horseradish

DRESSING

1 shallot, minced

3 tablespoons cider vinegar

3 tablespoons honey

2 tablespoons prepared horseradish

2 teaspoons Dijon mustard

½ cup (4 fl oz/125 ml) vegetable oil

salt and freshly ground pepper to taste

SLAW

4 cups (12 oz/375 g) mixed shredded
   red, green, and napa cabbages

2 apples, halved, cored, and grated

2 large carrots, peeled and grated

¼ cup (⅓ oz/10 g) chopped fresh
   flat-leaf (Italian) parsley

1 tablespoon caraway seeds (optional)

When the birch leaves turn yellow and the maple leaves turn red, the apples are ripe and the tiny town of Bayfield, Wisconsin, on the shore of Lake Superior, hosts its annual Applefest. Orchard men and women line Main Street selling their just-harvested apples and fresh cider, and church groups, sports teams, and charities sell home-baked apple pies, muffins, and cookies. This slaw, a mix of sweet apples, crisp cabbages, and a little tangy horseradish, is a taste of fall.

1. To make the dressing, in a blender or food processor, combine the shallot, vinegar, honey, horseradish, and mustard. With the motor running, add the oil in a slow, steady stream, processing until the mixture is emulsified and the consistency of heavy (double) cream. If it is too thick, thin with water. Season with salt and pepper.

2. To make the slaw, in a large bowl, toss together the cabbages, apples, carrots, and parsley. Add the dressing and toss well.

3. Sprinkle the slaw with the caraway seeds, if using, and serve. This may be made 1 day ahead, covered, and refrigerated.

SERVES 4–6

NUTRITIONAL ANALYSIS PER SERVING
Calories 304 (Kilojoules 1,277); Protein 2 g; Carbohydrates 28 g; Total Fat 22 g; Saturated Fat 3 g; Cholesterol 0 mg; Sodium 78 mg; Dietary Fiber 4 g

# Fresh Corn Pudding

¼ cup (½ oz/15 g) fresh bread crumbs

½ cup (2 oz/60 g) grated Colby cheese

8–10 large ears of corn, husks and silk removed

3 shallots, minced

1 cup (8 fl oz/250 ml) heavy (double) cream, lukewarm

3 dashes of Tabasco or other hot-pepper sauce

1 teaspoon salt

¼ teaspoon freshly ground pepper

6 eggs, lightly beaten

2 teaspoons chopped fresh thyme

boiling water, as needed

Toward the end of August, some people in the corn-growing states of Iowa, Minnesota, and Kansas actually get tired of eating corn. This recipe offers a comforting solution to too much of a good thing. Similar to a soufflé, the pudding puffs up, then sinks a little as it cools. It makes a stunning side dish as well as a simple main course when paired with heirloom tomatoes and crusty bread.

1. Preheat the oven to 350°F (180°C). Butter a 2-qt (2-l) soufflé dish or baking dish. Sprinkle with the bread crumbs and 2 tablespoons of the cheese and tilt to coat the bottom and sides evenly.

2. Resting an ear of corn on its stalk end in a shallow bowl, cut down along the ear with a sharp knife, stripping off the kernels and rotating the ear with each cut. Then run the flat side of the blade along the ear to remove any "milk." Repeat with as many ears as necessary until you have 4 cups (1½ lb/750 g) kernels. Set aside.

3. In a food processor, combine 1 cup (6 oz/190 g) of the corn, the shallots, cream, hot-pepper sauce, salt, and pepper. Process until creamy.

4. Turn the corn mixture into a large bowl and stir in the eggs, the remaining 3 cups (18 oz/560 g) corn, the thyme, and the remaining cheese. Pour into the prepared dish. To cover the dish, coat one side of a piece of aluminum foil generously with butter and place it, butter side down, over the dish. Put the dish in a baking pan and fill the pan with boiling water to reach two-thirds of the way up the sides of the baking dish.

5. Bake for 45 minutes. Remove the foil and continue baking until the pudding is lightly browned on top and a knife inserted into the center comes out clean, about 15 minutes longer.

6. Remove from the oven and serve immediately.

**SERVES 6–8 AS A SIDE DISH, OR 4 AS A MAIN COURSE**

NUTRITIONAL ANALYSIS PER SIDE-DISH SERVING
Calories 302 (Kilojoules 1,268); Protein 11 g; Carbohydrates 20 g; Total Fat 21 g; Saturated Fat 11 g; Cholesterol 238 mg; Sodium 479 mg; Dietary Fiber 3 g

# Heartland
# **Dairy**

The Heartland, which produces more than one-third of the nation's milk and almost all of its cheese and butter supply, continues to be America's dairy capital.

Until the mid–twentieth century, almost everyone in the rolling grassy hillsides of Wisconsin, Minnesota, and Iowa owned cows. Back then, families regularly churned butter for their own use and to sell through the nearby farmers' cooperative.

By the 1850s, dairy co-ops in the three major dairy states were supplying the country with butter. In 1924, the largest of these co-ops, Minnesota Cooperative Creameries Association, began branding its butter "Land O'Lakes." Today, this major food corporation processes over thirteen billion pounds (6.5 billion kg) of milk annually and markets more than six hundred dairy products across the United States and throughout the world.

The Heartland has also met the country's demand for organic butter. In 1990, the country's largest organic farmers' cooperative, CROPP, introduced the country's first organic cultured butter and organic salted butter under the brand name Organic Valley.

Today, these three dairy states produce almost 90 percent of the nation's butter, which continues to be the regional spread of choice.

The Heartland is also known for its cheese. It is home to Wisconsin's Colby, Iowa's Maytag blue, and Ohio's Liederkranz. Wisconsin, Minnesota, and Illinois alone produce over 90 percent of the cheese made in the United States today, and dramatic industry consolidation over the last seventy years has meant that large corporations now dominate supermarket shelves with their consistent products.

At the same time, small-scale cheese makers are growing in number. These entrepreneurs have found expanding markets in co-ops and specialty shops for their farmstead and raw-milk European-style cheeses.

But cheese has long played an important role in the Heartland economy. Wisconsin's first "native" cheese was Colby, which is similar to a mild cheddar but lower in acid and unaged. Iowa's famed Maytag blue is made only from the milk of Holsteins. Liederkranz, a soft, pungent cheese, has been made in Van Weit, Ohio, for over seventy-five years. The washed-rind cow's milk cheese is creamy, slightly salty, and strong.

More traditional European-style cheeses, such as Gouda, Havarti, and Tilsit, are being made in small batches with organic milk throughout the region. In addition, some of the country's most interesting goat's and sheep's milk cheeses are being made on small farms in the Heartland, where products run the gamut from unripened chèvres to a wide variety of aged specialties.

Organic milk, butter, and a variety of artisan cow's, goat's, and sheep's milk cheeses produced in the Heartland.

# Tomatoes with Goat Cheese–Basil Dressing

**DRESSING**

1 large shallot, chopped

2 tablespoons chopped fresh flat-leaf
(Italian) parsley

2 teaspoons white wine vinegar

¼ cup (2 fl oz/60 ml) mayonnaise

2 oz (60 g) creamy fresh goat cheese

3 tablespoons milk, or as needed

salt and freshly ground pepper to taste

1 head green or red leaf lettuce,
separated into leaves

3 lb (1.5 kg) mixed heirloom tomatoes
*(see note),* sliced or, if cherry
tomatoes, quartered

1 cup (1 oz/30 g) fresh basil leaves,
cut into narrow strips

Among summer's great luxuries are vine-ripened tomatoes.
Try blending mellow, mild varieties, such as the heirloom
Zebra, Rutgers, and Beefsteak, with dramatic tart-sweet
ones, such as Sweet 100s and Sun Gold, for a full spectrum
of tastes on one big plate.

1. To make the dressing, in a blender, combine the shallot, parsley, and
vinegar and process until puréed. Add the mayonnaise, goat cheese, and
3 tablespoons milk and process until smooth and creamy. Add more milk
as needed to thin to the correct consistency. Season with salt and pepper.

2. Line a large platter or individual salad plates with the lettuce leaves.
Arrange the tomatoes on the leaves and sprinkle with the basil. Drizzle
some of the dressing evenly over the tomatoes, then pass the remaining
dressing at the table.

SERVES 6–8

NUTRITIONAL ANALYSIS PER SERVING
Calories 132 (Kilojoules 554); Protein 4 g; Carbohydrates 11 g; Total Fat 9 g;
Saturated Fat 2 g; Cholesterol 9 mg; Sodium 99 mg; Dietary Fiber 3 g

The tomatoes you remember eating as a child, sun-ripened and splitting with juice, are being grown once again by small-scale farmers and market gardeners, thanks to such organizations as Seed Savers Exchange, a nonprofit group based in Decorah, Iowa. Dedicated to promoting the cultivation of vegetables and fruits no longer considered commercially viable because they do not ship well, Seed Savers works to reclaim precious seeds threatened with extinction.

The eight thousand members of Seed Savers grow and distribute to the public the seeds for heirloom vegetables, fruits, and grains. They focus primarily on seeds brought to North America by immigrant gardeners and farmers and on the traditional varieties grown by Native Americans, Mennonites, and Amish. Since its founding in 1975, Seed Savers, through its Seed Exchange program, has distributed an estimated 750,000 samples of endangered seeds.

The Heritage Farm, the organization's scenic 170-acre (70-hectare) headquarters near Decorah, is a living museum of historic fruit, vegetable, and grain varieties. In the education center, a display of endangered food

# Seed **Savers** Exchange

crops is maintained. Each summer, some five thousand gardeners, farmers, and orchardists tour the facilities, including the most diverse public orchard in the country, home to many now-rare varieties of North American apples and grapes. In the adjoining gardens, more than eighteen thousand rare vegetable varieties are being maintained and multiplied for seed.

# Perfect Green Beans

1–1¼ lb (500–625 g) green beans, trimmed

2–3 tablespoons walnut, hazelnut (filbert), or extra-virgin olive oil

1–2 teaspoons coarse salt, or to taste

2 tablespoons chopped toasted walnuts (optional)

No fancy tricks here, just be sure to cook these beans until tender to coax forth their full flavor (tender-crisp is not enough). I use coarse salt, as fine salt can coat the beans too thoroughly, making them overly salty. Hazelnut, walnut, and extra-virgin olive oil all contribute a unique flavor. Choose the one you like best.

1. Bring a large saucepan three-fourths full of water to a rolling boil. Add the beans and cook until tender, about 5 minutes.

2. Drain the beans and place in a shallow dish. While still warm, toss the beans with the oil and sprinkle with the salt. Scatter the walnuts over the beans, if desired. Serve warm or at room temperature.

SERVES 4–6

NUTRITIONAL ANALYSIS PER SERVING
Calories 89 (Kilojoules 374); Protein 2 g; Carbohydrates 6 g; Total Fat 7 g; Saturated Fat 1 g; Cholesterol 0 mg; Sodium 447 mg; Dietary Fiber 2 g

# Apple, Hickory Nut, and Cheddar Salad

¼ cup (1 oz/30 g) hickory nuts or pecans

¼ cup (2 fl oz/60 ml) red wine vinegar

1 tablespoon Dijon mustard

¾ cup (6 fl oz/180 ml) extra-virgin olive oil

pinch of sugar, or to taste

salt and freshly ground pepper to taste

2 heads butter (Boston), Bibb, red or green leaf lettuce, or a combination

2 tart apples such as Haralson, Cortland, or McIntosh, unpeeled, halved, cored, and sliced ¼ inch (6 mm) thick

¼ lb (125 g) Wisconsin cheddar, crumbled

This simple salad is a shining example of Wisconsin-style regional flavors: sharp cheddar, tart apples, and delicate hickory nuts in a lusty red wine vinaigrette. Hickory nuts are wild pecans, sweeter and earthier than their commercial cousins. They grow throughout the Midwest and are sold at farmers' markets and specialty-foods stores and through mail-order catalogs.

1. Preheat the oven to 400°F (200°C). Place the nuts on a baking sheet and toast, stirring, until they begin to darken and release their fragrance, about 10 minutes. Remove and set aside.

2. In a small bowl, whisk together the vinegar and mustard. Whisk in the olive oil until well blended. Whisk in the sugar, salt, and pepper.

3. Tear the lettuce leaves into bite-sized pieces and place in a large bowl. Add the apples, cheese, and nuts and toss briefly to combine. Add the dressing and toss again to coat.

4. Arrange the salad on chilled individual salad plates and serve immediately.

SERVES 6–8

NUTRITIONAL ANALYSIS PER SERVING
Calories 337 (Kilojoules 1,415); Protein 5 g; Carbohydrates 10 g; Total Fat 32 g; Saturated Fat 7 g; Cholesterol 17 mg; Sodium 158 mg; Dietary Fiber 2 g

# Spinach Soufflé

1 lb (500 g) spinach, stems removed

½ cup (2 oz/60 g) chopped yellow
onion

1 tablespoon water

5 tablespoons (2½ oz/75 g) unsalted
butter

4 tablespoons (1 oz/30 g) grated
Parmesan cheese

¼ cup (1½ oz/45 g) all-purpose
(plain) flour

1½ cups (12 fl oz/375 ml) milk,
heated

6 eggs, separated

2 pinches of salt

pinch of freshly ground black pepper

pinch of cayenne pepper

This recipe makes showy and easy use of the plentiful eggs produced on Midwest farms. Use organic eggs if possible, as the true flavor of a good egg shines in this simple dish.

1. In a saucepan, combine the spinach, onion, and water. Cover, place over medium-low heat, and cook until the spinach is bright green and tender, about 4 minutes. Drain the spinach mixture, pressing out any liquid. Chop and set aside.

2. Preheat the oven to 400°F (200°C). Butter a 2-qt (2-l) soufflé dish or four 2-cup (16–fl oz/500-ml) individual soufflé dishes. Sprinkle the inside of the dish(es) with about 1 tablespoon of the cheese, tilting to coat the bottom and sides evenly.

3. In a saucepan over medium heat, melt the remaining butter. When it foams, add the flour and reduce the heat to medium-low. Cook, stirring, until the mixture darkens a bit, about 3 minutes. Whisk in the milk a little at a time, whisking vigorously after each addition to prevent lumps. When all of the milk has been added, cook over low heat, whisking, until thick, 1–2 minutes longer. Remove from the heat.

4. In a small bowl, beat together the egg yolks, a pinch of salt, the black pepper, cayenne pepper, and the remaining 3 tablespoons cheese. Stir into the milk. Add the spinach mixture and stir to combine.

5. In a bowl, beat the egg whites with a pinch of salt until they hold stiff peaks. Stir a couple of spoonfuls of the beaten egg whites into the egg yolk–milk mixture to lighten it. Using a rubber spatula, gently fold in the remaining whites. Transfer the batter to the prepared dish(es).

6. Bake until the soufflé has risen and is browned on top, 30–40 minutes or 15–18 minutes if using individual soufflé dishes. Use a knife to check the interior; it should be a little moist. If still wet, bake for another 5 minutes. Serve immediately.

SERVES 4–6

NUTRITIONAL ANALYSIS PER SERVING
Calories 306 (Kilojoules 1,285); Protein 15 g; Carbohydrates 13 g; Total Fat 22 g; Saturated Fat 12 g; Cholesterol 301 mg; Sodium 271 mg; Dietary Fiber 2 g

# Pickled Red and Gold Beets

1 lb (500 g) each red and gold beets, peeled

1 white onion, sliced

1 clove garlic, sliced

1 cup (8 fl oz/250 ml) cider vinegar

¼ cup (2 oz/60 g) sugar, or to taste

1 tablespoon cardamom seeds

1 tablespoon whole cloves

1 tablespoon ground allspice

pinch of salt

1. Put the red beets and the gold beets into separate saucepans and add water to cover by 2 inches (5 cm). Bring to a boil over high heat, reduce the heat to medium-low, cover partially, and simmer until tender, 25–30 minutes. Drain, reserving 2 cups (16 fl oz/500 ml) of the cooking liquid from the gold beets. Let cool slightly.

2. When the beets are cool enough to handle, cut into slices ¼ inch (6 mm) thick and divide them and the onion and garlic slices evenly between 2 sterilized 1-qt (1-l) canning jars.

3. In a saucepan, combine the reserved 2 cups (16 fl oz/500 ml) beet juice, the vinegar, sugar, cardamom, cloves, allspice, and salt. Place over medium heat and heat, stirring, just long enough to dissolve the sugar, then pour over the beets, immersing them fully and filling the jars to within ¼ inch (6 mm) of the top. Using a hot, damp towel, wipe the rims clean. Seal tightly with lids and screw bands. Process the jars in a hot-water bath for 15 minutes. Using tongs, transfer to a cooling rack, let cool to room temperature, and check for a good seal. Label and store in a cool, dark place for up to 3 months. If the seal is not good, store in the refrigerator for up to 1 week.

MAKES 2 QT (2 L)

# Cranberry-Ginger Relish

1. Using a vegetable peeler or zester, remove the zest from the orange and place in a food processor. Slice the orange in half and squeeze the juice into the food processor.

2. Pick over the cranberries, discarding any bruised ones, and add to the processor along with the crystallized and fresh ginger and the ½ cup (4 oz/125 g) sugar. Process until the mixture is chunky, 15–30 seconds. Taste and add more sugar, if desired. Transfer to a serving dish. The relish will keep, covered and refrigerated, for up to 1 month.

MAKES ABOUT 1 QT (1 L)

1 large orange

4 cups (1 lb/500 g) cranberries

¼ cup (1½ oz/45 g) crystallized ginger, chopped

2 teaspoons peeled and grated fresh ginger

½ cup (4 oz/125 g) sugar, or to taste

Putting up jams, jellies, pickles, and butters with backyard and woodland bounty is an annual event in many Heartland homes. Stocking the larder and at the same time making enough for gift giving is a traditional kitchen project that marks the end of summer. But folks who have neither the time nor the know-how to put up their own foods readily turn to the growing number of regional purveyors.

One such company is Petosky, Michigan's American Spoon Foods, which turns the finest of the state's foodstuffs into a line of flavorful preserves, sauces, and dressings. Founded by Justin Rashid and Larry Forgione, the chef of An American Place in New York City and an active promoter of regional foods, the company is named after its first preserves, a batch so loaded with strawberries that a spoon was needed to scoop the luscious fruit from the jar. Delicious pumpkin butter, cherry-gooseberry relish, cranberry maple syrup, and thimbleberry preserves are among the company's products.

Another local purveyor is Northland Native Products in Minneapolis, which sells food gathered by Native Americans and processed according

# Canning and **Preserving**

to traditional methods. Their wild rice is harvested by hand from natural rice beds along the shore of nearby Leech Lake. A line of wild-fruit jellies—chokecherry, plum, hawthorn berry, currant—is made from recipes calling for little sugar, while maple and wild berry syrups are produced in small batches without additives or preservatives.

# Pepper and Corn Relish

about 8 ears of corn, husks and silk removed

3 red (Spanish) onions, finely chopped

2 green bell peppers (capsicums), seeded and finely chopped

1 red bell pepper (capsicum), seeded and finely chopped

1 orange bell pepper (capsicum), seeded and finely chopped

2 tomatoes, peeled, seeded, and chopped

½ cup (4 oz/125 g) sugar

1 tablespoon salt

1 tablespoon mustard seeds

½ teaspoon freshly ground pepper

½ cup (4 fl oz/125 ml) fresh apple cider or apple juice

This condiment goes particularly well with grilled hot dogs, hamburgers, and chicken.

1. Resting an ear of corn on its stalk end in a shallow bowl, cut down along the ear with a sharp knife, stripping off the kernels and rotating the ear with each cut. Repeat with as many ears as necessary until you have 3 cups (18 oz/560 g) kernels.

2. In a preserving kettle or other large, heavy pot, combine the corn, onions, bell peppers, tomatoes, sugar, salt, mustard seeds, pepper, and cider. Bring to a boil over high heat, reduce the heat to medium-low, and simmer, stirring occasionally, until the corn is tender and bright, 10–15 minutes.

3. Spoon the relish into hot sterilized canning jars to within ¼ inch (6 mm) of the top. Using a hot, damp towel, wipe the rims clean. Seal tightly with lids and screw bands. Process the jars in a hot-water bath for 15 minutes. Using tongs, transfer to a cooling rack, let cool to room temperature, and check for a good seal. Label and store in a cool, dry place for up to 3 months. If the seal is not good, store in the refrigerator for up to 1 week.

**MAKES ABOUT 2 QT (2 L)**

NUTRITIONAL ANALYSIS PER ¼ CUP (60 ML) SERVING
Calories 40 (Kilojoules 168); Protein 1 g; Carbohydrates 9 g; Total Fat 0 g; Saturated Fat 0 g; Cholesterol 0 mg; Sodium 223 mg; Dietary Fiber 1 g

# Braised Red Cabbage with Ginger

To set the vibrant red of the cabbage, toss it with vinegar before cooking, a culinary tip passed down through generations of Midwest farmwives of Eastern European ancestry who made creative use of their bountiful cabbage harvest. Fresh and crystallized ginger give this classic recipe a pleasant spicy kick. Any leftovers are great the next day on grilled Reuben sandwiches.

1. In a large, deep saucepan over medium heat, melt the butter. Add the onion and sauté until translucent, 5–7 minutes.

2. In a large bowl, toss the cabbage with the vinegar, then add it to the pan along with the apples and the crystallized and fresh ginger. Cook over medium heat until the cabbage begins to wilt, about 5 minutes.

3. Add the cider, brown sugar, salt, and pepper. Cover, reduce the heat to low, and cook until the cabbage is tender, about 10 minutes. Taste and adjust the seasoning.

4. Transfer to a serving dish and serve hot or at room temperature.

SERVES 6

NUTRITIONAL ANALYSIS PER SERVING
Calories 159 (Kilojoules 668); Protein 3 g; Carbohydrates 31 g; Total Fat 5 g;
Saturated Fat 2 g; Cholesterol 10 mg; Sodium 29 mg; Dietary Fiber 5 g

2 tablespoons unsalted butter

1 small yellow onion, thinly sliced

1 head red cabbage, shredded

¼ cup (2 fl oz/60 ml) cider vinegar

2 tart apples, peeled, halved, cored, and thinly sliced

1 tablespoon crystallized ginger, chopped

2 teaspoons peeled and minced or grated fresh ginger

¼ cup (2 fl oz/60 ml) fresh apple cider

2–3 tablespoons brown sugar, or to taste

salt and freshly ground pepper to taste

# Summer Greens with Hazelnuts and Berries

1 small red (Spanish) onion, thinly
sliced

¼ cup (1½ oz/45 g) hazelnuts (filberts)

6 oz (185 g) mixed salad greens
*(see note)*

1 cup (4 oz/125 g) sliced strawberries

salt and freshly ground pepper to taste

VINAIGRETTE
¼ cup (2 fl oz/60 ml) raspberry
vinegar

1 shallot, chopped

1 teaspoon Dijon mustard

½ cup (4 fl oz/125 ml) hazelnut
(filbert) oil or extra-virgin olive oil

¼ cup (1 oz/30 g) raspberries,
crushed

pinch of sugar, or to taste

This salad is best made with a mix of salad greens and herbs: slightly bitter curly endive (chicory), peppery dandelion, lemony sorrel, and anise-scented chervil. Lamb's lettuce (sometimes called corn salad because it grows between corn rows) is a small, hardy plant with dark, tender leaves on short stems. It is especially good in salads with fruit. Any leftover dressing will keep in the refrigerator, covered, for up to 2 days.

1. In a bowl, combine the onion slices with ice water to cover.

2. Preheat the oven to 350°F (180°C). Spread the nuts on a baking sheet and toast until the skins begin to darken and crack, about 10 minutes. Remove from the oven, wrap the still-warm nuts in a clean kitchen towel, and rub them between your palms to remove the skins. Chop and set aside.

3. To make the vinaigrette, in a small bowl, whisk together the vinegar, shallot, and mustard. Whisk in the oil. Stir in the raspberries and sugar.

4. Drain the onion slices. In a large bowl, combine the greens, strawberries, and onion, and toss with enough dressing to coat lightly. Season with salt and pepper and toss again. Sprinkle the hazelnuts over the salad and serve.

**SERVES 6**

NUTRITIONAL ANALYSIS PER SERVING
Calories 232 (Kilojoules 974); Protein 2 g; Carbohydrates 7 g; Total Fat 23 g;
Saturated Fat 2 g; Cholesterol 0 mg; Sodium 32 mg; Dietary Fiber 2 g

# Farmers'
# **Markets**

Farmers' markets bring the taste of the country to town. Set up in vacant parking lots, alleyways, and pedestrian malls, farmers' markets allow urban dwellers to purchase fresh produce from the farmers who have grown it, many of them recent immigrants.

The Heartland's farmers' markets have long been seedbeds of change, steadily shifting portraits of demographic and culinary trends. Early Norwegian immigrants sold potatoes, while their Italian counterparts introduced tomatoes and squashes. Later, Mexican American farmers lit our taste for chiles. Today's Amish and Mennonite farmers, descendants of nineteenth-century religious and social reformers who settled in the area to escape persecution, sell their produce and bundles of culinary and medicinal herbs, all harvested without the use of contemporary tools.

The most recent wave of significant immigration began in the 1980s. Newly arrived Hmong and Vietnamese immigrants planted the foods of their homelands, introducing exotic chiles and herbs to the marketplace and sharing their passion for hot, sour, and bitter flavors. They have made cilantro (fresh coriander) nearly as popular as parsley and have brought bitter melon, lotus root, and lemongrass to the Midwestern table.

In the 1990s, Somali and Tibetan refugees added their flavors to the Heartland markets in Minneapolis and St. Paul, Detroit, Chicago, Des Moines, Cleveland, Milwaukee, and Madison. Draped in brightly colored fabric, Somali women harvest bitter greens and grind spicy peanut sauces and sell them to adventurous shoppers. Tibetans have expanded the availability of different grades of basmati and jasmine rice, and the once-narrow definition of curry has been broadened to include the intensely spiced dishes of these newcomers.

Not all of the farmers at the stalls have grown their produce in countryside fields. The Hmong, refugees from northern Laos, have proved to be extraordinary urban farmers. At the end of the Vietnam War, some twelve thousand Hmong left their mountain villages, trekked to neighboring Thai refugee camps, and then were flown to Minneapolis, St. Paul, Detroit, and Chicago. They were given access to unbuildable tracts of city land that bordered railroads and highways. Masterly farmers, they were soon leasing market stalls and

piling them high with purple-tinged basil; fat, twisted radishes; and searing hot chiles. They grew American staples, too, such as sugar snap peas, stocky cabbages, and leafy lettuces.

On a busy market morning, Hmong teenagers dressed in blue jeans handle the money and explain to customers how to use their families' harvests of exotic ingredients in a simple soup or stir-fry.

Produce from Midwest farmers' markets reflects the diverse cultural influences of the Heartland table: red cabbage, potatoes, onions, beets, parsley, and dill (opposite); lemongrass, bok choy, ginger, and cilantro (below).

# Fresh Succotash Salad

about 8 ears of corn, husks and silk removed, or about 3 cups (18 oz/560 g) frozen kernels

1 cup (7 oz/220 g) fresh or frozen shelled soybeans

1 pt (12 oz/375 g) cherry tomatoes, stems removed and halved

1 red bell pepper (capsicum), seeded and cut into ¼-inch (6-mm) dice

3 green (spring) onions, including 3 inches (7.5 cm) of green tops, thinly sliced

2 tablespoons fresh lime juice

½ teaspoon Dijon mustard

1 small clove garlic, minced

½ teaspoon sugar

¼ teaspoon curry powder

¼ cup (2 fl oz/60 ml) olive oil

2 tablespoons chopped fresh cilantro (fresh coriander)

2 tablespoons chopped fresh basil

1 tablespoon chopped fresh mint

salt and freshly ground pepper to taste

In this version of succotash, lima beans are replaced with young soybeans, which are pale, vibrant green, and sweeter than limas. The Midwest grows one-third of the world's soybean supply. Fresh soybeans are sold in their green pods and, for this recipe, will need to be shelled and briefly cooked. If fresh soybeans are unavailable, substitute frozen ones, or use fresh or frozen baby lima beans. If frozen vegetables are used, reduce the blanching time to 30 seconds.

1. If using fresh corn, rest an ear on its stalk end in a shallow bowl and cut down along the ear with a sharp knife, stripping off the kernels and rotating the ear with each cut. Repeat with as many ears as necessary until you have 3 cups (18 oz/560 g) kernels.

2. Bring a large saucepan three-fourths full of water to a boil. Add the soybeans and corn kernels and blanch for 1 minute. Drain immediately and plunge into ice water to stop their cooking. Drain well.

3. In a large bowl, toss together the soybeans, corn kernels, tomatoes, bell pepper, and green onions.

4. In a small bowl, whisk together the lime juice, mustard, garlic, sugar, and curry powder. Whisk in the olive oil. Pour over the vegetables and toss to coat evenly.

5. Add cilantro, basil, and mint and season with salt and pepper. Toss again and serve at once.

SERVES 4–6

NUTRITIONAL ANALYSIS PER SERVING
Calories 370 (Kilojoules 1,554); Protein 18 g; Carbohydrates 38 g; Total Fat 20 g; Saturated Fat 3 g; Cholesterol 0 mg; Sodium 38 mg; Dietary Fiber 10 g

# Horseradish Mashed Potatoes

4 lb (2 kg) baking potatoes, peeled
and cut into 4-inch (10-cm) chunks

1 teaspoon salt

½ cup (4 oz/125 g) unsalted butter,
at room temperature

1 cup (8 fl oz/250 ml) milk, heated

1 tablespoon freshly grated
horseradish or 2 teaspoons
prepared horseradish, or to taste

salt and freshly ground pepper to taste

Fresh horseradish is a pungent, spicy white root that grows like a weed in many Midwest backyard gardens. Here, it enlivens creamy potatoes. Leave a few lumps in the potatoes for texture, a sign that the dish is homemade, and, for variety, stir in mashed cooked turnips, parsnips, or rutabagas. Serve these potatoes with Blue Plate Meat Loaf (page 62).

1. In a large pot, combine the potatoes with water to cover by about 2 inches (5 cm). Add the salt and bring to a boil over medium-high heat. Cook, uncovered, until tender, 20–30 minutes.

2. Drain the potatoes, return them to the pot, and set over low heat. Using a potato masher, mash the potatoes, adding the butter and milk as you mash. Once the milk and butter are fully incorporated, mix in the horseradish, salt, and pepper.

3. Transfer to a warmed serving bowl and serve at once.

SERVES 6–8

NUTRITIONAL ANALYSIS PER SERVING
Calories 292 (Kilojoules 1,226); Protein 5 g; Carbohydrates 37 g; Total Fat 14 g;
Saturated Fat 9 g; Cholesterol 40 mg; Sodium 196 mg; Dietary Fiber 3 g

# Roasted Beets with Maytag Blue Cheese

Sweet, earthy beets pair beautifully with this pungent, creamy blue cheese from Iowa. Maytag blue was developed by Frederick Maytag, grandson of the washing-machine mogul, to make use of the milk from his father's prize-winning Holstein cows. The big, well-ripened wheels are divided into wedges with special cutters fashioned from old washing machines.

1. Preheat the oven to 350°F (180°C).

2. If the beet greens are still attached, cut them off, leaving about 1 inch (2.5 cm) of the stems intact. Prick the beets with a fork or sharp knife, but do not peel. Place on an ungreased baking sheet and roast until tender when poked with a sharp knife, about 1 hour. Remove from the oven and set aside until cool enough to handle.

3. While the beets are roasting, in the bottom of a serving bowl, whisk together the vinegar, Worcestershire sauce, garlic, pepper, and rosemary. Whisk in the olive oil.

4. Using your fingers, slip the peels off the beets, then slice the beets into wedges about 1 inch (2.5 cm) thick. Add the wedges to the balsamic mixture, toss to coat evenly, and let cool to room temperature.

5. Sprinkle the crumbled cheese over the beets and serve at room temperature.

**SERVES 4**

NUTRITIONAL ANALYSIS PER SERVING
Calories 331 (Kilojoules 1,390); Protein 4 g; Carbohydrates 10 g; Total Fat 32 g;
Saturated Fat 7 g; Cholesterol 11 mg; Sodium 257 mg; Dietary Fiber 1 g

4 or 5 beets, about 1 lb (500 g) total weight

¼ cup (2 fl oz/60 ml) balsamic vinegar

dash of Worcestershire sauce

2 cloves garlic, minced

1 teaspoon freshly cracked pepper

1 tablespoon chopped fresh rosemary

1 cup (4 fl oz/125 ml) extra-virgin olive oil

2 oz (60 g) crumbled Maytag or other blue cheese

# Cracked Wheat Salad with Asparagus

## SALAD

3 cups (24 fl oz/750 ml) water

1 teaspoon salt, plus salt to taste

1 cup (6 oz/185 g) cracked wheat

1 lb (500 g) asparagus, tough stem ends removed

1 pt (12 oz/375 g) cherry tomatoes, stems removed and halved or quartered lengthwise

6 green (spring) onions, white part only, chopped

¼ cup (⅓ oz/10 g) chopped fresh basil

¼ cup (⅓ oz/10 g) chopped fresh cilantro (fresh coriander)

2 tablespoons chopped fresh mint

2 tablespoons chopped fresh flat-leaf (Italian) parsley

freshly ground pepper to taste

## VINAIGRETTE

½ teaspoon grated lemon zest

2 tablespoons fresh lemon juice

1 tablespoon chopped fresh mint

1 tablespoon chopped fresh cilantro (fresh coriander)

1 tablespoon chopped fresh flat-leaf (Italian) parsley

1 clove garlic, minced

½ teaspoon sugar

⅓ cup (3 fl oz/80 ml) extra-virgin olive oil

Cracked wheat, dried wheat berries that have been broken into rough pieces, makes a deliciously nutty addition to salads and an interesting substitute for rice. Although similar in appearance to bulgur, which is first steamed and then dried and has its bran partially removed before crushing, cracked wheat is not as delicate and has a more distinct wheat flavor.

1. In a saucepan, bring the water and the 1 teaspoon salt to a rapid boil over high heat. Add the cracked wheat, reduce the heat to medium, and simmer, uncovered, until tender, 30–45 minutes. Drain and set aside.

2. Bring a saucepan three-fourths full of water to a boil. Cut the asparagus into 2-inch (5-cm) pieces. Add to the boiling water and cook until tender-crisp and bright green, 3–5 minutes. Drain and plunge into ice water to stop the cooking. Drain again. Reserve the tips for garnish.

3. To make the vinaigrette, in a small bowl, whisk together the lemon zest, lemon juice, mint, cilantro, parsley, garlic, and sugar. Whisk in the olive oil.

4. In a large bowl, toss together the cooked cracked wheat, the asparagus, tomatoes, green onions, basil, cilantro, mint, and parsley. Toss with the vinaigrette to coat. Season with salt and pepper and serve.

SERVES 4–6

NUTRITIONAL ANALYSIS PER SERVING
Calories 286 (Kilojoules 1,201); Protein 8 g; Carbohydrates 35 g; Total Fat 16 g; Saturated Fat 2 g; Cholesterol 0 mg; Sodium 485 mg; Dietary Fiber 9 g

# Wild Rice Pilaf with Ramps and Mushrooms

1 tablespoon unsalted butter

4 ramps or 1 small leek, white part only, chopped

1 lb (500 g) mixed fresh mushrooms such as white button, shiitake, morel, and wood ear, brushed clean or rinsed if laden with grit

1 cup (6 oz/185 g) wild rice, rinsed and drained

¼ cup (⅓ oz/10 g) chopped fresh flat-leaf (Italian) parsley

salt and freshly ground pepper to taste

Although cultivated wild rice is widely available, use the hand-harvested lake rice if you can find it, as it has a particularly light and delicate flavor. Ramps, which grow wild throughout the Midwest, have an intense garlic-onion flavor. Look for them in the springtime at farmers' markets or specialty-foods stores.

1. In a saucepan over medium heat, melt the butter. Add the ramps or leek and the mushrooms and sauté until the leek or ramps are translucent and the mushrooms begin to brown, about 8 minutes.

2. Add the wild rice, parsley, salt, pepper, and water to cover by 1 inch (2.5 cm). Bring to a boil, reduce the heat to low, cover, and cook until the wild rice is tender, about 45 minutes. Drain off any excess water. The cooking time will vary with different batches of rice. The wild rice is ready when the grains puff up and the inner, lighter part is visible. Overcooking increases the volume but turns the rice mushy.

3. Transfer to a warmed serving dish and serve.

SERVES 6

NUTRITIONAL ANALYSIS PER SERVING
Calories 146 (Kilojoules 613); Protein 6 g; Carbohydrates 27 g; Total Fat 2 g; Saturated Fat 1 g; Cholesterol 5 mg; Sodium 7 mg; Dietary Fiber 3 g

Heartlanders are serious foragers of all kinds of wild foods. In Michigan and Minnesota, morel gatherers are obsessively protective of their hunting grounds, insisting guests be blindfolded before setting out. In mid- to late May, these honeycombed mushrooms poke up through dead leaves and out from under oak stumps. They taste of loam and the damp woods. Split the stems and rinse under running water to dislodge the grit.

Ramps, sometimes called wild leeks, are prized by many of today's restaurant chefs for their assertive flavor. Resembling green (spring) onions with lilylike leaves, they sprout in fields and on the borders of forests. Split them as you would a leek and rinse under running water to clean.

Fiddleheads are pale green baby ferns shaped like the scroll of a violin. Wild asparagus push their heads up through the cool earth in early May. They are wonderful combined in a quick sauté.

Hickory nuts flourish from central Wisconsin through Missouri. They have an extraordinarily hard shell, the cracking of which requires a hammer swung with considerable

# Wild **Harvest**

force. Although wonderfully rich and buttery, hickory nuts have never been harvested commercially because of their steel-tough shells.

Wild huckleberries, which resemble tiny blueberries, grow on thick, low bushes in the northern Heartland. They have small, hard seeds, thick skins, and a tart flavor. They are usually cooked into jams and jellies.

Mitchell's
PERSIMMON
FESTIVAL
SEPT. 23-30

# 4 Desserts

In this land of sweet butter and cream, high-quality wheat, wild berries, and flourishing orchards, dessert is inevitably a treat. The Heartland's lofty chiffon cakes, deep-dish fruit pies, and puffy oven pancakes are made to be served with coffee, traditionally a light roast (aka Swedish gasoline) consumed in multiple cupfuls at a sitting. Wisconsin invented the ice cream sundae as a sinfully delicious after-church sweet, while few and tedious are the region's civic meetings that don't include a plate of cookies or toothsome bars.

# Sour Cream–Brown Sugar Cookies

1 cup (7 oz/220 g) firmly packed brown sugar

½ cup (4 oz/125 g) unsalted butter, at room temperature

1 egg

1 teaspoon vanilla extract (essence)

2½ cups (12½ oz/390 g) all-purpose (plain) flour

1 teaspoon baking powder

¼ teaspoon baking soda (bicarbonate of soda)

½ teaspoon salt

½ cup (4 oz/125 g) sour cream

¼ cup (2 oz/60 g) granulated sugar

These old-fashioned cookies are as essential on the farm as a tractor. Grab a handful, a big glass of cold lemonade, and a book and go sit for a while under the shade of a tree. Sour cream makes these cookies soft, moist, and tangy. Bake an extra batch to freeze for another day.

1. Preheat the oven to 375°F (190°C). Lightly butter baking sheets or line with parchment (baking) paper.

2. In a large bowl, using an electric mixer set on medium-high speed, beat together the brown sugar and butter, stopping often to scrape down the sides of the bowl, until creamy, 1–2 minutes. Beat in the egg and vanilla.

3. In another bowl, sift together the flour, baking powder, baking soda, and salt. Add the flour mixture in 3 batches to the butter mixture alternately with the sour cream, beginning and ending with the flour mixture and mixing well after each addition.

4. Have ready a small shallow bowl filled with water and a second bowl holding the granulated sugar. Drop the dough by rounded teaspoonfuls 3 inches (7.5 cm) apart onto the prepared sheets. Dip the bottom of a flat juice glass into the water, and then into the sugar, and lightly press on each mound of dough to form a round about 2 inches (5 cm) in diameter.

5. Bake the cookies, 2 sheets at a time, rotating and switching the sheets at midpoint, until the cookies are golden brown and set, 10–12 minutes. Transfer the cookies to racks to cool. Store in airtight containers for up to 1 week or freeze for up to 1 month.

**MAKES 4–5 DOZEN COOKIES**

NUTRITIONAL ANALYSIS PER COOKIE
Calories 64 (Kilojoules 269); Protein 1 g; Carbohydrates 10 g; Total Fat 2 g; Saturated Fat 1 g; Cholesterol 10 mg; Sodium 40 mg; Dietary Fiber 0 g

# Lemon Chiffon Cake

2¼ cups (9 oz/280 g) cake (soft-wheat) flour

1½ cups (12 oz/375 g) sugar

½ teaspoon baking soda (bicarbonate of soda)

½ teaspoon salt

½ cup (4 fl oz/125 ml) vegetable oil

7 whole eggs, separated, plus 3 egg whites

⅔ cup (5 fl oz/160 ml) water

3 tablespoons fresh lemon juice

3 tablespoons grated lemon zest

1 teaspoon vanilla extract (essence)

1¼ teaspoons cream of tartar

Under the banner of Betty Crocker, this type of recipe was hailed as "the first new type of cake in one hundred years, as glamorous as the angel food cake, but easier to make." General Mills purchased the recipe in the 1950s from Harry Baker, who created elegant desserts for Hollywood stars when he was not busy at his full-time job of selling insurance. Rich yet light, lemon chiffon is an American classic. Serve with lightly sweetened, whipped heavy (double) cream, if you like.

1. Preheat the oven to 325°F (165°C).

2. In a large bowl, sift together the flour, sugar, baking soda, and salt. Make a well in the center, then add the vegetable oil, egg yolks, water, lemon juice, lemon zest, and vanilla extract. Using a whisk, beat all of the ingredients together until smooth, about 1 minute.

3. Place the 10 egg whites in another large bowl. Using an electric mixer, beat on high speed until frothy. Add the cream of tartar and continue beating until soft peaks form. Using a rubber spatula, gently fold the egg whites into the batter just until no white streaks remain. Pour the batter into an ungreased 10-inch (25-cm) tube pan.

4. Bake the cake until a toothpick inserted into the center comes out clean and the top springs back when lightly pressed in the center, 55–60 minutes. Remove from the oven and invert the pan, placing the tube opening over the neck of a bottle to suspend it over the counter. Let cool completely in the pan, about 2 hours.

5. Lift the pan off the bottle, then run a long knife around the inside edge of the pan to loosen the cake from the pan sides. Turn the cake out of the pan, and place it on a serving plate. Using a serrated knife, cut into wedges to serve.

**SERVES 12–14**

NUTRITIONAL ANALYSIS PER SERVING
Calories 294 (Kilojoules 1,235); Protein 6 g; Carbohydrates 43 g; Total Fat 11 g; Saturated Fat 2 g; Cholesterol 114 mg; Sodium 185 mg; Dietary Fiber 0 g

# Milling and
# **Flour**

The Heartland has long been the world's bread basket and continues to supply the nation with flour. More than 40 million acres (16 million hectares) of the region's farmland are devoted to wheat fields, producing some 80 million bushels (28 million hectoliters) of raw wheat.

When it comes to processing the Heartland's wheat, today's entrepreneurial millers are going back to the grindstone. The retro technology yields a gray flour speckled with bran, germ, and oil that many bakers appreciate for its high nutritive value and wheaten flavor. It's a full retreat from the roller technology that revolutionized milling and introduced to the public downy white Gold Medal Flour, the nation's first choice for over seventy years.

The milling industry was founded in the 1800s by two strong rivals, Charles Pillsbury of Pillsbury Company and Cadwallader Washburn of Washburn-Crosby Company, which was later to become General Mills. Washburn introduced steel rollers from Hungary and successfully ground the area's prolific hard red wheat into pure white flour with fewer "impurities" than grindstones had achieved. This strain of wheat, which grows in Kansas and Nebraska through the winter and in the Dakotas through the spring, yields a low-moisture, high-gluten flour that makes exceptional bread. (Interestingly, the middlings, small, unprocessed clumps of wheat endosperm discarded in the milling process, became the basis for Cream of Wheat, the nation's oldest packaged hot cereal.)

Not everyone was eager to embrace pure white flour, however. Sylvester Graham, a contemporary of Washburn and Pillsbury and a Presbyterian minister, denounced the roller millers for "putting asunder what God has joined together" and pre-scribed whole wheat as essential to a healthy, godly diet. Inspired by Graham, Dr. John Harvey Kellogg, at a sanatorium in Battle Creek, Michigan, put his patients on a whole-grain regimen, which marked the beginning of the now-famous line of Kellogg breakfast cereals.

Eventually, people came to under-stand that less-processed flour was more nutritious. By the 1940s, scien-tists confirmed the health benefits of whole-wheat (wholemeal) flour, and consumers pressured companies to refortify white flour with niacin, iron, and vitamins $B_1$ and $B_2$.

Today's small-scale millers, such as Hodgson Mills, in Teutopolis, Illinois, and Little Bear in Winona, Minnesota, have returned to grindstones as a way of producing more nutritious products naturally. They generally mill an unbleached all-purpose (plain) flour, bread flour ground from hard red wheat berries high in gluten, and whole-wheat or graham flour.

The Heartland is home to millers big and small, producing a variety of flours from all-purpose white to stone ground whole wheat (opposite). Saint Lucia's Day Coffee Bread (below and page 133) is the perfect anytime snack.

# Deep-Dish Apple-Blueberry Pie

Pastry dough (page 28)

1½ pt (12 oz/375 g) blueberries

2 apples, peeled, halved, cored, and
  cut into ½-inch (12-mm) pieces

½ cup (4 oz/125 g) sugar, or to taste

Make this pie early in the fall when the new apples are tart and the late-season blueberries are slightly overripe and very sweet. Wild or low-bush blueberries are smaller and snappier than cultivated high-bush berries. They grow along the rocky shores of northern lakes and throughout the boggy woods.

1. Prepare the pastry dough and chill as directed.

2. Preheat the oven to 350°F (180°C).

3. On a floured pastry cloth or waxed paper, roll out half of the dough into a 13-inch (33-cm) round about ⅛ inch (3 mm) thick. Drape around the rolling pin and carefully transfer to a 9-inch (23-cm) deep-dish pie pan, pressing it gently into the bottom and sides of the pan. Trim the edge, leaving a ½-inch (12-mm) overhang.

4. In a large bowl, gently toss together the blueberries, apples, and sugar. Pour into the pastry-lined pie pan.

5. On a lightly floured pastry cloth or waxed paper, roll out the remaining dough and transfer to the top of the pie in the same way. Press firmly around the edges to seal the crusts together, trimming away any excess overhang, then fold the overhang under itself all around and flute the edge attractively. Make 3 slashes 2 inches (5 cm) long in the pastry.

6. Bake the pie until the crust is golden brown and firm and the juices have bubbled through the slashes, 50–60 minutes. Transfer to a rack to cool for 15–20 minutes. Serve warm or at room temperature.

SERVES 8–10

NUTRITIONAL ANALYSIS PER SERVING
Calories 368 (Kilojoules 1,546); Protein 6 g; Carbohydrates 60 g; Total Fat 12 g;
Saturated Fat 7 g; Cholesterol 75 mg; Sodium 265 mg; Dietary Fiber 3 g

# Old-Fashioned Sundae with Fresh Cherries

ICE CREAM

3½ cups (28 fl oz/875 ml) heavy (double) cream

1 cup (8 fl oz/250 ml) milk

1 cup (8 oz/250 g) sugar

½ vanilla bean, or 2 teaspoons vanilla extract (essence)

CHOCOLATE SAUCE

6 oz (185 g) semisweet (plain) chocolate, chopped, or chocolate chips

½ cup (4 fl oz/125 ml) strong brewed coffee

½ teaspoon vanilla extract (essence)

CHERRIES

1 cup (4 oz/125 g) cherries, pitted

2 tablespoons sugar, or to taste

Two Rivers, Wisconsin, was home to the original sundae, created in 1881 by Ed Berners in his tiny ice-cream parlor when a customer requested chocolate sauce on his dish of vanilla ice cream. The recipe for this ice cream, made with cream but not eggs, is easy because the base doesn't need to be cooked.

1. To make the ice cream, in a large bowl, combine the cream, milk, and sugar. If using the ½ vanilla bean, split it lengthwise and, using the tip of a knife, scrape the seeds into the cream mixture. If using vanilla extract, add it to the cream mixture. Stir to dissolve the sugar and mix the ingredients thoroughly. Cover and refrigerate for at least 2 hours or for up to overnight.

2. Pour the cream mixture into an ice-cream maker and freeze according to the manufacturer's instructions.

3. To make the sauce, combine the chocolate and coffee in the top pan of a double boiler placed over simmering water in the lower pan. Heat, stirring often, until melted and smooth. Remove from over the water and stir in the vanilla.

4. To prepare the cherries, in a small saucepan over low heat, stir together the cherries and sugar. Warm just until the sugar melts. Do not allow the cherries to cook.

5. To serve, scoop the ice cream into large tumblers or bowls. Crown each serving with a few cherries and spoon the warm sauce over the top.

SERVES 6–8

NUTRITIONAL ANALYSIS PER SERVING
Calories 703 (Kilojoules 2,953); Protein 5 g; Carbohydrates 59 g; Total Fat 53 g; Saturated Fat 32 g; Cholesterol 168 mg; Sodium 66 mg; Dietary Fiber 2 g

# Cranberry Sorbet

2 cups (8 oz/250 g) cranberries

½ cup (4 fl oz/125 ml) cranberry or cranberry-apple juice

1½ cups (10½ oz/330 g) superfine (caster) sugar

Tangy and light and a brilliant magenta, this sorbet is wonderful after a big meal. Be sure you taste the cranberry mixture before freezing, as each batch of fruit varies in tartness. Eat the sorbet as soon as possible after making it. The ideal soft, creamy consistency doesn't last long.

1. In a small saucepan over medium-low heat, combine the cranberries and cranberry or cranberry-apple juice and heat, stirring occasionally, until the cranberries pop, 5–7 minutes. Stir in the sugar until it dissolves. Remove from the heat, let cool, cover, and refrigerate until well chilled, about 2 hours.

2. Pour the cranberry mixture into an ice-cream maker and freeze according to the manufacturer's instructions.

3. Scoop into bowls to serve.

**SERVES 4**

NUTRITIONAL ANALYSIS PER SERVING
Calories 334 (Kilojoules 1,403); Protein 0 g; Carbohydrates 86 g; Total Fat 0 g; Saturated Fat 0 g; Cholesterol 0 mg; Sodium 2 mg; Dietary Fiber 2 g

M ove over Cape Cod. Wisconsin is now the largest producer of cranberries in the world, supplying an average of 300 million pounds (150 million kg) each season, which is about half of the national crop. The cranberries come to market in mid-September, just as summer's berries are dwindling. A bit paler and larger than New England's deep red berries, Wisconsin cranberries give relishes and baked goods a punch of flavor.

Cranberries, native to North America, flourish in acidic sandy bogs. Native Americans harvested the wild berries and used them for food, dye, and medicine. Most likely named for the wild cranes that are at home in the same bogs, the plants, which are perennials, are now cultivated in beds that can remain in steady production for a hundred years.

The colorful harvest draws over forty thousand people to the Cranberry Festival in Warrens, Wisconsin (population three hundred). Shaken from their canes, or woody stems, by machines resembling enormous eggbeaters, the berries float on flooded bogs, creating a scarlet circle in a field of sky-blue water. Wooden frames, called booms, sweep the

# Wisconsin **Cranberries**

berries into huge black vacuum tubes that suck them onto a conveyor belt that then spills them into a truck.

The cranberry's most familiar role in the kitchen is in the making of sauces. For the best results, cook cranberries until their skins pop before adding any sugar, as berries cooked with sugar from the beginning often develop tough skins.

# Apple Oven Pancake with Berries and Lemon

¼ cup (2 oz/60 g) unsalted butter

3 eggs

¾ cup (6 fl oz/180 ml) milk

¾ cup (4 oz/125 g) all-purpose (plain) flour

1 teaspoon vanilla extract (essence)

1 teaspoon grated lemon zest

1 tart apple such as Cortland or McIntosh, unpeeled, halved, cored, and thinly sliced

½ cup (4 fl oz/125 ml) heavy (double) cream

1 lemon, halved and one-half thinly sliced

2 tablespoons confectioners' (icing) sugar

1 pt (8 oz/250 g) raspberries

*Pfannkuchen,* a simple German oven pancake that is puffy and light on the outside and custardy within, is great for breakfast or dessert. Drizzle it with fresh lemon juice as it comes hot from the oven, then top with fresh berries and a little whipped cream.

1. Preheat the oven to 400°F (200°C).

2. In an ovenproof frying pan over high heat, melt the butter. Remove from the heat and set aside.

3. In a bowl, whisk together the eggs and milk until well blended. Whisk in the flour a little at a time, whisking until fully incorporated after each addition. Then whisk in the vanilla, lemon zest, and 2 tablespoons of the melted butter. Let the batter stand for about 10 minutes.

4. Return the frying pan with the remaining butter to high heat and melt the butter. Swirl it around to coat the bottom and sides of the pan and remove from the heat. Pour the batter into the pan. Arrange the apple slices in a circular pattern on top.

5. Bake the pancake for about 15 minutes. Reduce the oven temperature to 350°F (180°C) and continue baking until the pancake is puffy and the edges are golden, 10–15 minutes longer.

6. While the pancake is baking, in a bowl, whisk the cream until soft peaks form. Cover and refrigerate until needed.

7. When the pancake is ready, remove from the oven and slide from the pan onto a large platter. Squeeze the juice from 1 lemon half over the pancake, then, using a sieve or sifter, sift the confectioners' sugar evenly over the top. Scatter the berries over all. Cut into 4 wedges and garnish with the whipped cream and lemon slices. Serve at once.

SERVES 4

NUTRITIONAL ANALYSIS PER SERVING
Calories 463 (Kilojoules 1,945); Protein 11 g; Carbohydrates 44 g; Total Fat 29 g; Saturated Fat 16 g; Cholesterol 238 mg; Sodium 84 mg; Dietary Fiber 5 g

# Pound Cake with Rhubarb-Strawberry Sauce

POUND CAKE

1 cup (5 oz/155 g) all-purpose (plain) flour

⅛ teaspoon baking powder

grated zest of 1 orange

3 eggs

1 cup (8 oz/250 g) sugar

⅛ teaspoon salt

¼ cup (2 fl oz/60 ml) heavy (double) cream

½ cup (4 oz/125 g) unsalted butter, melted and cooled

¼ cup (1 oz/30 g) chopped black walnuts

RHUBARB-STRAWBERRY SAUCE

about 8 rhubarb stalks, trimmed and cut into ½-inch (12-mm) pieces (4 cups/1¼ lb/625 g)

1 cup (8 oz/250 g) sugar

juice of 1 orange

1 pt (8 oz/250 g) strawberries, stems removed and sliced

Toast any leftover cake slices the next morning, and spread with a little jam for a breakfast treat. The accompanying rhubarb-strawberry sauce is also delicious on ice cream, pancakes, or waffles.

1. Preheat the oven to 325°F (165°C). Butter an 8½-by-4½-by-2½-inch (21.5-by-11.5-by-6-cm) loaf pan. Dust with flour and tap out the excess.

2. To make the cake, in a bowl, sift together the flour and baking powder. Stir in the orange zest.

3. In a large bowl, using an electric mixer on high speed, beat together the eggs, sugar, and salt until thickened and pale, about 2 minutes. Reduce the speed to low and add the flour mixture in 3 batches alternately with the cream and melted butter, beginning and ending with the flour mixture and mixing well after each addition. Fold in the walnuts. Scrape the batter into the prepared pan.

4. Bake the cake until the top is golden and a knife inserted into the center comes out clean, 65–70 minutes. Transfer to a rack to cool in the pan for 15 minutes, then invert onto the rack and let cool completely.

5. While the cake is cooling, prepare the sauce: In a saucepan, combine the rhubarb and sugar and let stand until the rhubarb exudes some juice, about 10 minutes. Bring the mixture to a boil over medium-high heat, stirring constantly. Reduce the heat to low, add the orange juice, and simmer, stirring occasionally, until the rhubarb is tender and the liquid is thickened, 10–15 minutes. Remove from the heat and let cool to room temperature.

6. Gently stir the strawberries into the cooled sauce. Slice the cake and serve each slice topped with some sauce.

SERVES 8–10

NUTRITIONAL ANALYSIS PER SERVING
Calories 438 (Kilojoules 1,840); Protein 5 g; Carbohydrates 69 g; Total Fat 17 g; Saturated Fat 9 g; Cholesterol 109 mg; Sodium 68 mg; Dietary Fiber 1 g

# Wild Rice Pudding with Dried Cranberries

2 cups (16 fl oz/500 ml) milk

2 eggs

½ cup (5½ fl oz/170 ml) maple syrup

¼ cup (2 oz/60 g) firmly packed
brown sugar

¼ teaspoon freshly grated nutmeg

1½ cups (10 oz/315 g) cooked wild
rice

½ cup (2 oz/60 g) dried cranberries

1 teaspoon vanilla extract (essence)

pinch of salt

Sweetened with maple syrup and studded with dried fruit, this pudding plays on the flavors of the north woods. The recipe makes delicious use of leftover cooked wild rice. If you don't have any left over, cook a fresh batch: rinse ¾ cup (4½ oz/140 g) wild rice, place in a small saucepan with water to cover by 2 inches (5 cm), bring to a boil, reduce the heat to low, and cook, uncovered, until the grains are tender and just cracked open, about 45 minutes, then drain.

1. In the top pan of a double boiler, combine the milk, eggs, maple syrup, brown sugar, and nutmeg. Place over simmering water in the lower pan and heat until blended. Stir in the wild rice and cranberries. Cook, stirring constantly, until the mixture thickens just enough to coat a spoon lightly, about 7 minutes. Do not allow it to come to a boil, or the mixture will curdle.

2. Remove the pan from over the water and stir in the vanilla and salt. Transfer the pudding to a glass or ceramic serving dish and serve at once. Or, cover with plastic wrap, pressing it directly onto the surface to prevent a skin from forming, refrigerate, and serve chilled.

**SERVES 6**

NUTRITIONAL ANALYSIS PER SERVING
Calories 256 (Kilojoules 1,075); Protein 7 g; Carbohydrates 48 g; Total Fat 5 g; Saturated Fat 2 g; Cholesterol 82 mg; Sodium 92 mg; Dietary Fiber 1 g

W ild rice is not true rice, but the seed of an aquatic grass that grows along lakeshores in Wisconsin, Minnesota, and Canada. The Ojibway tribe of the Northland area of Minnesota has long considered the grain a dietary staple. For years, everyone in the tribal villages moved to rice camps along the lakeshore to participate in the harvest.

The Ojibway still hand-harvest the rice from canoes: one person poles the canoe, while two others knock the stalks into the boat. Back on shore, the rice is parched on screens over low fires, then threshed in small batches. The Ojibway regard the rice as sacred, and thus refuse to propagate it. The rice grows within the boundaries of the tribe's reservations. It's a big area and a big tribe, and only tribe members can harvest on that land.

Hand-harvested rice is lighter, more flavorful, and cooks more quickly than the cultivated wild rice that is also grown in Minnesota and Wisconsin. Although more expensive than brown or white rice, it swells up to four times its size when cooked, making it a good value if cost per serving is considered. Scandinavian

## Wild **Rice**

homesteaders called wild rice "pocket money," because a small amount expanded enough to feed a family of five.

Cook wild rice only until it puffs and splits to reveal the inner, lighter interior of the seed. Overcooking increases the volume but leaves the rice mushy. Uncooked wild rice can be stored in an airtight container in a cool place for several months.

# Raspberry Meringue Pinch Pie

## MERINGUE CRUST

6 egg whites, at room temperature

⅛ teaspoon cream of tartar

pinch of salt

½ cup (4 oz/125 g) sugar

2 teaspoons vanilla extract (essence)

1 cup (4 oz/125 g) ground almonds

1 tablespoon cornstarch (cornflour)

## FILLING

3 pt (1½ lb/750 g) red raspberries

2 tablespoons sugar

2 cups (16 fl oz/500 ml) heavy (double) cream

1 pt (8 oz/250 g) red or black raspberries

Lofty confections of crisp meringue, whipped cream, and lots of fresh berries, pinch pies are so named for the way the "crust" is pinched up to hold the filling. In areas of Wisconsin first settled by Germans, these same creations are known by their German name, *Schaumtorte,* and are served filled with any of a number of seasonal fruits—strawberries, blueberries, peaches, cherries, cranberries.

1. Preheat the oven to 225°F (110°C). Butter a baking sheet, then dust with flour, tapping off the excess.

2. To make the meringue crust, in a bowl, using an electric mixer, beat together the egg whites, cream of tartar, and salt until stiff but not dry. Gently fold in the sugar and vanilla. In a small bowl, stir together the almonds and cornstarch. Fold into the egg whites just until combined.

3. Spoon the meringue onto the prepared baking sheet and, using the back of a spoon or a spatula, spread it into a 10-inch (25-cm) round about 2 inches (5 cm) thick. Using your fingers and a spoon, pinch up the sides to make a rim 1 inch (2.5 cm) high.

4. Bake the meringue until well dried and barely golden, 1½–2 hours. Turn off the oven, partially open the door, and leave the meringue inside until it is cool and ready to use.

5. To make the filling, in a bowl, lightly crush the 3 pt (1½ lb/750 g) red raspberries and mix with the sugar. In a bowl, using the electric mixer or a whisk, beat the cream until soft peaks form. Fold the crushed raspberries into the whipped cream.

6. Pile the raspberry cream into the shell and scatter the 1 pt (8 oz/250 g) red or black raspberries on top. Serve immediately or refrigerate and serve within the hour.

**SERVES 6–8**

NUTRITIONAL ANALYSIS PER SERVING
Calories 510 (Kilojoules 2,142); Protein 9 g; Carbohydrates 43 g; Total Fat 35 g; Saturated Fat 17 g; Cholesterol 96 mg; Sodium 106 mg; Dietary Fiber 8 g

# Chocolate-Glazed Honey-Nut Bars

**BOTTOM LAYER**

2 cups (10 oz/315 g) all-purpose (plain) flour

⅔ cup (2½ oz/75 g) confectioners' (icing) sugar

pinch of salt

1 cup (8 oz/250 g) chilled unsalted butter

**TOP LAYER**

¾ cup (6 oz/185 g) unsalted butter

⅓ cup (4 oz/125 g) honey

½ cup (3½ oz/105 g) firmly packed brown sugar

2 tablespoons sour cream

2 cups (8 oz/250 g) chopped nuts such as pecans, walnuts, or almonds

1 cup (6 oz/185 g) semisweet (plain) chocolate chips

Honeybees feast on the clover, buckwheat, sassafras, and wild flowers that blossom in the Heartland's rolling green fields. The honey they produce reflects the flavor of their chosen meal. Clover is sweet and light, buckwheat is dark and almost molasseslike, sassafras has a licorice undertone, and wild flower is fragrant and mild. Choose the type you prefer for making these bars.

1. Preheat the oven to 350°F (180°C). Lightly butter a 9-by-13-inch (23-by-33-cm) baking pan.

2. To make the bottom layer, in a bowl, sift together the flour, sugar, and salt. Using 2 knives or your fingers, work in the butter until pea-sized pieces form. Alternatively, sift the flour, sugar, and salt into a food processor, add the butter, and pulse until pea-sized pieces form. Turn the flour mixture into the prepared pan and pat down lightly and evenly with your hands.

3. Bake until firm and golden, 15–20 minutes. Remove from the oven.

4. Meanwhile, make the top layer: In a small saucepan over medium-high heat, combine the butter, honey, brown sugar, and sour cream and heat, stirring, until the butter is melted and the ingredients are blended. Bring to a boil and cook until thickened, 1–2 minutes. Stir in the nuts.

5. Spread the top layer evenly over the bottom layer and return the pan to the oven. Bake until firm and puffy on top, about 20 minutes. Transfer the pan to a rack.

6. Place the chocolate in the top pan of a double boiler placed over hot water and heat, stirring, until melted and smooth. Drizzle the chocolate over the bars as they cool. Let the bars cool completely, then cut into diamonds, rectangles, or squares. Store in a cool place, wrapped in plastic or in an airtight container, for up to 5 days.

**MAKES 6–7 DOZEN BARS**

NUTRITIONAL ANALYSIS PER BAR
Calories 93 (Kilojoules 391); Protein 1 g; Carbohydrates 8 g; Total Fat 7 g; Saturated Fat 3 g; Cholesterol 11 mg; Sodium 3 mg; Dietary Fiber 0 g

# Persimmon Cake

½ cup (4 oz/125 g) unsalted butter, at room temperature

1 cup (8 oz/250 g) granulated sugar

1 egg

2 cups (8 oz/250 g) cake (soft-wheat) flour

1 teaspoon baking powder

1 teaspoon ground cinnamon

½ teaspoon baking soda (bicarbonate of soda)

½ teaspoon salt

½ teaspoon ground allspice

¼ teaspoon ground cloves

¼ teaspoon freshly grated nutmeg

1¼ cups (12½ oz/390 g) mashed persimmon pulp (fresh or canned)

½ cup (3 oz/90 g) dried currants

2 tablespoons confectioners' (icing) sugar

Persimmons grow wild along the southern tier of the Heartland, ripening early in the fall. Wild persimmons are small and red, similar in shape and flavor to the large, orange cultivated Hachiya variety. When ready to eat, they are very soft and have a mild, sweet flavor, somewhat like fresh apricots, while unripe, they are bitter. If fresh persimmons are unavailable, look for canned persimmon pulp in some specialty-foods stores or mail-order catalogs.

1. Preheat the oven to 350°F (180°C). Butter a 9-by-13-inch (23-by-33-cm) cake or baking pan, then dust with flour, tapping out the excess.

2. In a large bowl, using an electric mixer set on high speed, beat the butter until light and lemon colored, about 1 minute. Beat in the granulated sugar until creamy, about 3 minutes. Then beat in the egg until incorporated.

3. In another bowl, sift together the flour, baking powder, cinnamon, baking soda, salt, allspice, cloves, and nutmeg. Add the flour mixture in 3 batches to the butter mixture alternately with the persimmon pulp and beginning and ending with the flour mixture and mixing well after each addition. Fold in the currants. Pour into the prepared pan.

4. Bake the cake until it springs back when lightly pressed in the center, about 45 minutes. Transfer to a rack and let cool completely in the pan. Using a sieve or sifter, sift the confectioners' sugar evenly over the top. Cut into squares to serve.

SERVES 12–16

NUTRITIONAL ANALYSIS PER SERVING
Calories 242 (Kilojoules 1,016); Protein 2 g; Carbohydrates 43 g; Total Fat 7 g; Saturated Fat 4 g; Cholesterol 34 mg; Sodium 169 mg; Dietary Fiber 1 g

# Saint Lucia's Day Coffee Bread

Saint Lucia, a symbol of light and hope in many Swedish homes, is honored on December 13, once thought to be the longest and darkest night of the year. Inspired by the traditional Saint Lucia buns sold throughout the Christmas season in Midwest bakeries, this sunny gold loaf takes less time to make. Serve it warm out of the oven, or slice it the next day, spread it with a little apricot jam, and accompany it with a cup of coffee.

1. Preheat the oven to 350°F (180°C). Butter a 9-by-5-inch (23-by-13-cm) loaf pan.

2. In a bowl, stir together the flour, sugar, baking powder, and salt. In a small bowl, stir together the milk, orange zest, and saffron. Beat in the egg and butter.

3. Make a well in the center of the flour mixture and pour the milk mixture into it. Using a large spoon or rubber spatula, combine the ingredients swiftly, stirring and folding rather than beating. Stop as soon as all the dry ingredients are moistened. The batter should be lumpy, not smooth. Gently stir in the raisins. Scrape the batter into the prepared pan.

4. Bake the bread until a toothpick inserted into the center comes out clean, 55–60 minutes. Let cool in the pan on a rack for about 10 minutes before turning out of the pan. Serve warm or at room temperature.

**SERVES 8–10**

NUTRITIONAL ANALYSIS PER SERVING
Calories 373 (Kilojoules 1,567); Protein 8 g; Carbohydrates 69 g; Total Fat 8 g;
Saturated Fat 5 g; Cholesterol 44 mg; Sodium 507 mg; Dietary Fiber 2 g

3 cups (15 oz/470 g) all-purpose
(plain) flour

⅔ cup (5 oz/155 g) sugar

4 teaspoons baking powder

1 teaspoon salt

1½ cups (12 fl oz/375 ml) milk

1 teaspoon grated orange zest

⅛ teaspoon saffron threads

1 egg

¼ cup (2 oz/60 g) unsalted butter,
melted and cooled

1 cup (6 oz/185 g) golden raisins
(sultanas)

# Poached Pears with Spiced Cream

6 pears such as Bartlett (Williams')
   or Seckel

1 cup (8 fl oz/250 ml) sweet white
   wine such as Riesling or Sauternes

½ cup (4 fl oz/125 ml) water

½–¾ cup (4–6 oz/125–185 g) sugar,
   or to taste

1 lemon, sliced

1 cinnamon stick

2 whole cloves

2 tablespoons heavy (double) cream

Pear trees flourish in many backyards and orchards across the Heartland, especially along the shores of Lake Superior and Lake Michigan. For this simple dessert, it's best if the pears are not too ripe. If you like, make this recipe ahead and serve the pears at room temperature or chilled.

1. Peel the pears, then core each pear from the blossom end with a melon baller, scooping the pear to within ½ inch (12 mm) of the stem, leaving the stem intact.

2. In a heavy saucepan large enough to hold all the pears upright, combine the wine, water, and ½ cup (4 oz/125 g) sugar and bring to a boil over medium heat, stirring to dissolve the sugar. Reduce the heat to medium-low and add the lemon, cinnamon stick, and cloves. Taste and add more sugar, if desired. Stand the pears, blossom end down, in the pan, cover, and simmer until the pears are soft when pierced with a sharp knife, about 20 minutes.

3. Using a slotted spoon, transfer the pears to a plate and tent with aluminum foil to keep warm. Raise the heat to high and cook the sauce until it is reduced by half, 10–15 minutes. Strain the sauce through a medium-mesh sieve. Swirl in the cream.

4. To serve, pour a little of the hot sauce onto individual plates and set a pear on each pool of sauce. Pass the remaining sauce at the table.

SERVES 6

NUTRITIONAL ANALYSIS PER SERVING
Calories 212 (Kilojoules 890); Protein 1 g; Carbohydrates 51 g; Total Fat 3 g;
Saturated Fat 1 g; Cholesterol 7 mg; Sodium 5 mg; Dietary Fiber 5 g

# Blue Ribbon Cinnamon Buns

## DOUGH

2½ teaspoons (1 package) active dry yeast

¼ cup (2 fl oz/60 ml) warm water (105°–115°F/41°–46°C)

2½ cups (12½ oz/390 g) all-purpose (plain) flour, or as needed

¼ cup (2 oz/60 g) granulated sugar

1 teaspoon salt

2 eggs, lightly beaten

¼ cup (2 fl oz/60 ml) milk

1 teaspoon vanilla extract (essence)

¼ cup (2 oz/60 g) unsalted butter, at room temperature

## FILLING

½ cup (3½ oz/105 g) firmly packed dark brown sugar

2 teaspoons ground cinnamon

1 teaspoon freshly grated nutmeg

## ICING

¼ lb (125 g) cream cheese, at room temperature

¼ cup (2 oz/60 g) unsalted butter, at room temperature

1 teaspoon vanilla extract (essence)

1–1¼ cups (4–5 oz/125–155 g) confectioners' (icing) sugar, sifted

pinch of salt

1. To make the dough, in a large bowl, sprinkle the yeast over the warm water and let stand until foamy, about 5 minutes. Using a wooden spoon, mix in ½ cup (2½ oz/75 g) of the flour, the granulated sugar, salt, eggs, milk, and vanilla until blended. Gradually stir in the remaining 2 cups (10 oz/ 315 g) flour until the dough comes together. Turn out the dough onto a lightly floured surface and knead until smooth and elastic, adding more flour if necessary to prevent sticking, 7–10 minutes. Knead in the butter until incorporated. Shape into a ball, place in a large buttered bowl, and turn to coat its surface with butter. Cover loosely with plastic wrap and let rise in a warm place until doubled in volume, about 1½ hours.

2. Punch down the dough, turn out onto a lightly floured surface, and knead briefly. Return the dough to the bowl, again cover loosely with plastic wrap, and again let rise until doubled, about 1 hour.

3. Butter a 9-by-13-inch (23-by-33-cm) baking pan. Punch down the dough and, on a floured surface, roll out into a 16-by-12-inch (40-by-30-cm) rectangle. To make the filling, mix together the brown sugar, cinnamon, and nutmeg. Sprinkle evenly over the rectangle. Starting from a long side, roll up as you would a jelly roll. Cut into 8 equal slices and arrange, cut side down, in the prepared pan. Cover loosely with plastic wrap and let rise until doubled, about 1 hour. Preheat the oven to 350°F (180°C).

4. Bake the rolls until golden, about 30 minutes. Meanwhile, prepare the icing: In a bowl, using an electric mixer, whip together the cream cheese and butter until light and fluffy. Beat in the vanilla, then gradually beat in the confectioners' sugar and salt until light and smooth.

5. Let the rolls cool in the pan on a rack for 5 minutes, then invert onto a platter and spread with the icing. Serve hot, warm, or at room temperature.

**MAKES 8 BUNS**

NUTRITIONAL ANALYSIS PER BUN
Calories 475 (Kilojoules 1,995); Protein 8 g; Carbohydrates 68 g; Total Fat 19 g; Saturated Fat 12 g; Cholesterol 103 mg; Sodium 379 mg; Dietary Fiber 1 g

In the Heartland, flaky pie crusts and delicate cakes have always been yardsticks of a cook's skills. But venture through the home arts pavilion at any Midwest state fair, and you'll find that the competition is not just about sweets. Since the 1800s, fair judges have been awarding blue ribbons in dozens of categories of homemade food, from baked goods to tart pickles and preserves, all made by entrants who have cooked their way through a series of qualifying rounds at the county, district, and regional levels.

Some national cooking contests are sponsored by major food corporations, including the Midwest's Pillsbury, General Mills, and Land O'Lakes, and the contest winners receive handsome prize money for their efforts. The first national baking competition was hosted by Pillsbury in Minneapolis in 1949, and soon became known simply as the Pillsbury Bake Off, the most renowned of all such contests. Over the years, the winning recipes have been published in a series of cookbooks that have helped shape the way we bake today.

A Tunnel of Fudge Cake, the 1966 winner, popularized the then little-known bundt pan. Some winning

# Blue **Ribbons**

recipes have had grocers scrambling to order special ingredients, such as the Starlight Mint Surprise cookies that cleaned out the supply of Mint Wafers in a single day.

The stakes are high at state fairs, too. Food producers often purchase winning recipes for jams, jellies, pickles, and preserves, then award the creator a residual on every jar sold.

# Glossary

### Apple Cider, Fresh

Sometimes called sweet cider or simply apple juice, fresh apple cider refers to unpasteurized, unfiltered apple juice and is used as an ingredient in recipes and as a beverage. It is not to be confused with hard, or alcoholic, cider, which is slightly fermented, resulting in a low alcohol content ranging from 3 to 7 percent. Ciders often contain the juice of several apple varieties, particularly Red Delicious, Jonathan, and McIntosh.

### Apples

John Chapman, America's legendary Johnny Appleseed, planted thousands of acres of apple orchards as he traveled on foot through the Heartland. Today, Michigan continues to be among the leading apple-producing states in the nation. Among the thousands of apple varieties that took root, a few remain particularly important. The deep red **Cortland** has a tangy-sweet flavor, making it an excellent apple for cooking—it breaks down nicely for applesauce—and for eating out of hand. Bright red, mildly tart **Haralson** apples, first grown in Minnesota, hold their shape and texture well during baking. The **McIntosh** is one of the most popular apples for both cooking and eating raw. Its juicy, crisp flesh has a spicy flavor and a fragrant aroma that recalls ripe berries. The attractive **Prairie Spy** is prized for its red-and-yellow skin, its juicy flesh, and its robust flavor. Excellent both for eating raw and for all-purpose cooking, it is also a good keeper, its flavor deepening with storage.

### Bacon

German immigrants brought their knowledge of raising pigs and smoking meats to the Heartland and quickly established bacon as a staple in Midwest kitchens. Made from the belly cut, which lies just below the spareribs, bacon is cured with salt and typically smoked. Most early smokehouses used smoldering hickory logs to provide the flavor for the meats hung from their eaves, and many cooks—and eaters—still consider fragrant hickory smoke ideal for bacon. Although presliced, plastic-wrapped bacon is widely available, look for **slab bacon,** which can be sliced as desired, for the best quality. **Canadian bacon,** or back bacon as it is known in Canada, comes from the loin along the back of the hog. Leaner, drier, and fully cooked, it has a mild flavor and meaty texture that is more similar to ham than to bacon. It is sold both presliced and in large pieces for slicing at home.

### Beets

Scandinavian and Eastern European immigrants discovered the cool temperatures of the Heartland brought out the crimson color and earthy sweetness of this root vegetable. Stored in root cellars or put up as pickles, beets provide Heartlanders with an essential vegetable through the long winters. Few potluck tables are complete without a deep red beet salad or a plate of jewel-tone pickles. Milder golden beets are now popular as well. They offer an even sweeter flavor but do not stain like their red cousins. For the best results, cook beets whole and unpeeled, then peel and cut as desired.

### Cabbage

Whether used raw in a tangy coleslaw for a picnic or barbecue, simmered in a soup for a hearty lunch, or cooked into a traditional sauerkraut for a family supper, this cruciferous vegetable is a staple of the Heartland table. **Napa cabbage,** also known as Chinese or celery cabbage, has long, pale yellow-green crinkly leaves, with wide, white veins. Its delicate texture and relatively loosely layered leaves make it ideal for using fresh as a wrapper around savory fillings. **Red cabbage,** with its deep color, thicker leaves, and slightly peppery flavor, is excellent for cooking and for adding raw to salads.

## Chile Sauce

This mild-flavored bottled sauce, made from tomatoes, sugar, vinegar, herbs, and spices such as chili powder or chiles, has the consistency of ketchup and is typically used as a table condiment.

## Fennel Bulb

Sweet and crisp, with a delicate anise flavor, fennel bulbs, also known as finocchio, resemble broad, tightly layered celery ribs topped with delicate, feathery leaves, or fronds. Native to the Mediterranean, and a popular item on Italian tables, the bulbs are enjoyed both raw and cooked. Florence fennel is the most widely available variety.

## Ginger

The rhizome of a tropical plant, ginger is prized around the world for its warm, citruslike flavor. Fresh ginger is grated or sliced and added to sauces, soups, and marinades to add a singular, refreshing note. Dried, finely ground ginger is an essential ingredient in the spiced cakes and cookies that northern Europeans introduced to the Heartland. Cooked in syrup and then coated with sugar, crystallized ginger adds a sweet-spicy accent to breads, fruit compotes, and desserts.

## Horseradish

Central European immigrants established horseradish farms in the rich Mississippi River basin of eastern Illinois. Long summers allowed excellent growth, and cold winters encouraged the dormancy required to develop the pungency of the gnarled, dark-skinned root. Once the creamy-white flesh is grated or ground, horseradish releases its characteristic mustardlike odor and flavor. Prepared horseradish is available widely, but it is worth finding the fresh root for its clean, sharp flavor.

## Maple Syrup

Maple syrup is produced from the boiled sap of the sugar maple tree, native to the northeastern Heartland. It is a favorite topping at the breakfast table, an ingredient in baking, and a thickener in sauces and glazes. Pure maple syrup is graded by color: Grade A Light, Medium, and Dark Ambers; and Grade B. Grade A Light Amber has the most delicate maple flavor and is the most popular choice for use as a topping; Grade B has an intense maple flavor and is often used in cooking.

# Herbs

### CILANTRO

Also known as fresh coriander and Chinese parsley, and popular in Latin American and Asian cooking, cilantro adds lemony pungency when used as an ingredient or a garnish.

### DILL

The feathery fronds of the dill plant are added to salads, pickles, and fish dishes to impart an aromatic tartness.

### MARJORAM

A slightly milder relative of oregano, marjoram is used fresh to bring out the flavors of tomatoes, legumes, lamb, poultry, or eggs.

### MINT

The refreshing flavor of mint brightens lamb and poultry dishes, vegetables, salads, and desserts. Although many varieties are cultivated, spearmint is the most readily available.

### ROSEMARY

Native to the Mediterranean, rosemary possesses an aromatic pine-lemon flavor that marries well with beans, soups, breads, potatoes, and roasted meats and poultry.

### SAGE

The mildly musty flavor of gray-green sage leaves adds depth to stews, stuffings, dairy and vegetable dishes, and roasted meats and poultry.

### TARRAGON

The narrow leaves of tarragon impart a fragrant sweetness and hints of anise flavor to eggs, vegetables, chicken, and fish.

## Mushrooms

Mushrooms grow in abundance in the dells of the Heartland, and foraging for them is a ritual after the cool rains of spring and autumn. A wide range of mushroom varieties appears in food stores. Widely cultivated and highly versatile in the kitchen, the familiar **white button mushroom** is mild but readily soaks up other flavors. Its close cousin, the **cremini mushroom,** also known as the common brown mushroom, is pale brown and has a slightly stronger flavor. If left to mature completely, cremini mushrooms become **portobello mushrooms,** prized for their large, meaty caps and rich, smoky flavor. The **morel mushroom** has an elongated, honey-combed cap and an intense muskiness that is highly valued in the Heartland and beyond. Beautiful, fan-shaped, pale gray **oyster mushrooms** have a silken texture and hints of shellfish flavor. The brown-capped **shiitake mushroom** is widely available both fresh and dried. Once dried, its flavor intensifies and its color darkens. Crinkled **wood ear mushrooms,** nearly always dried, have little flavor of their own but add crunchy texture to fillings and vegetable dishes.

## Nuts

Many types of nuts are important to the Heartland table. **Almonds,** commonly available skinned (blanched) and unskinned, are used in both sweet and savory dishes for their delicate flavor and elegant oval shape. The native **black walnut** has a stronger flavor than its more common English kin. Many cooks prefer black walnuts for their rich, slightly astringent flavor, although their hard shells make extracting the meats difficult. Small, round **hazelnuts,** also known as filberts, have a sweet, rich flavor. **Hickory nuts** (see also page 107), whose hard shells

are also a challenge to open, are small and buttery tasting. From the tallest member of the hickory family comes the popular **pecan,** a favorite nut throughout the region and the nation for pies, candies, ice creams, and fillings.

## Oils

While solid fats such as lard and vegetable shortening have a long history in the traditional cooking of the Midwest, healthier oils have replaced them in many contemporary kitchens. **Extra-virgin olive oil** from the Mediterranean is now standard in many salads and sauces. Because its fruity flavor breaks down when exposed to high heat, its use on the stove top should be limited. Richly flavored **hazelnut** and **walnut oils,** many of them of produced in France and Italy, add depth to sauces, dressings, and desserts. Because of their low smoke points, they are unsuitable for most cooking. To keep them fresh, store in tightly sealed containers in the refrigerator.

## Parsnips

The long, tapering, ivory-colored parsnip root becomes increasingly starchy and fibrous as it ages. Select smaller, younger parsnips for the sweetest flavor and most tender texture. Parsnips are excellent puréed or roasted. They are at their best during the cold months, when wintertime frost turns their starches to sugar.

## Pears

Succulent pears sweeten the Heartland table primarily during the fall and winter months. **Bartlett pears,** also known as Williams' pears, will soften and ripen to either a lightly speckled yellow or a deep red. They have the generous curves and musky perfume associated with classic holiday fruits. The tiny **Seckel** pear, sugary sweet and dark green

with a blush of maroon, has become a favorite for desserts and preserves.

## Rhubarb

Each spring in the upper Heartland, rhubarb plants send up bright red stalks and large leaves. Although it is a vegetable, rhubarb is generally treated as a fruit, and its assertively tart flavor mellows when cooked with sugar. It is a classic pie filling, especially when paired with strawberries, and its ruby hue ensures attractive jams and jellies. The plant's heart-shaped leaves are mildly toxic and should always be discarded. In grocery stores, the scarlet stalks are trimmed and sold in bunches like celery. Select the thinnest, reddest stalks for the best flavor and color.

## Rutabagas

Sometimes called a yellow turnip, this rugged root vegetable of fall and winter offers firm, substantial starch with a sweet flavor. Developed in Sweden by crossing a turnip with a cabbage, rutabagas are also known as Swedish turnips or swedes. Their flesh is denser and sweeter than that of turnips. They are excellent puréed, roasted, or stewed. Their tough skins must be thickly peeled and the cut pieces rubbed with lemon juice to prevent discoloring.

## Stout

First brewed in the British Isles, stout is a type of ale that uses deep-roasted barley to gain a dark, almost black color and a pronounced roasted, grainy flavor. Many Midwestern microbreweries (see page 71) now offer their own versions of this rich beer.

## Tomatoes

Once drained, the moist lowlands stretching from Ohio through Illinois were ideal for growing tomatoes, and newer varieties were quickly developed for these reclaimed stretches. Large, dense **Beefsteak** tomatoes are a favorite for slicing in sandwiches and cooking down in sauces. Reliable **Sweet 100s** and golden yellow **Sungold** have become two of the most popular cherry tomato varieties. Home gardeners prize the large, bright red, slightly flattened **Rutgers** tomato for both slicing and canning. It has thick walls, few seeds, and low acidity. The striking green-on-yellow streaks of the **Zebra** tomato make this small, sweet-tart variety one of the most beautiful for eating raw.

## Turnips

A staple in northern Europe, turnips adapted well to the rugged conditions of the Heartland prairies. The most familiar varieties of this root vegetable are large and white, with a tinge of purple at their stem ends. Tender and sweet when young, turnips become woodier and stronger in flavor as they age. The roots are excellent puréed and in stews and soups.

## Vinegar

Left to nature, fermented liquids will develop into an acidic solution. **Cider vinegar,** made from apple cider or apple cores, was a staple on frontier farms. It was essential for preserving food for the cellar, and its fruity tartness was also enjoyed at the table as a condiment or in desserts as a substitute for rare lemons. Vinegars from around the world fill the modern Heartland pantry. Rich, mellow, sweet **balsamic vinegar** from Italy appears in salads and sauces. Delicate **champagne** and **raspberry vinegars** are excellent in vinaigrettes and in lighter sauces for fish or poultry. **Red wine** and **white wine vinegars** add depth to sauces, stews, and marinades.

# Spices

**ALLSPICE, GROUND**

The berry of a tropical evergreen tree, allspice possesses a complex flavor that hints at cinnamon, nutmeg, and cloves. It appears in both sweet and savory cooking.

**CARDAMOM**

Related to ginger, the highly aromatic pods of the cardamom plant hold tiny black seeds that have a warm, sweet flavor. Native to India, it is also widely used in Scandinavian cuisine, especially fruit dishes and baked desserts.

**CARAWAY SEEDS**

These small, curving, brown seeds give rye bread its characteristic nutty, anisey flavor. A popular spice in the German pantry, caraway is used to flavor meats, cabbage, sausages, cheese, and breads.

**FENNEL SEEDS**

The pale, striped seeds of the fennel plant add a gentle licorice flavor to savory and sweet dishes, from sausages, stews, and roasts to breads, desserts, and liqueurs.

**NUTMEG**

The warm, sweet flavor of freshly grated nutmeg complements creamy sauces and desserts, baked treats, and vegetables such as potatoes and winter squash.

**PAPRIKA**

A bright red powder ground from the pepper (capsicum) of the same name. A popular ingredient in Hungarian cooking, paprika is used to flavor sauces, braises, or stews or as a colorful garnish on finished dishes. Two basic types, sweet and hot, are the most widely available.

**PEPPERCORNS, BLACK AND GREEN**

The tiny fruit of a tropical vine, the peppercorn delivers piquant heat to savory dishes around the world. Black peppercorns are fruits harvested when slightly underripe and then dried. Green peppercorns are the same fruits but harvested at an earlier stage. They are available dehydrated or packed in water or brine.

**SAFFRON THREADS**

Golden-hued saffron threads are the highly prized, handpicked stigmas of a particular purple crocus. A small amount will infuse soups, sauces, breads, and rice dishes with a deep yellow hue and earthy flavor.

# Index

## Acknowledgments

Leigh Beisch wishes to thank Northland Native American Products, Payson Fruit Growers, and Seed Savers Exchange.

Weldon Owen wishes to thank the following people and associations for their generous assistance and support in producing this book:
Desne Border, Ken DellaPenta, Jana Lee, Kathy Schermerhorn, Stephanie Sherman, and Hill Nutrition Associates.

## Photo Credits

Weldon Owen wishes to thank the following photographers and organizations for permission to reproduce their copyrighted photographs:
(Clockwise from top left) Pages 14–15 : Envision/B.W. Hoffmann, Tony Stone Images/Andy Sacks, Bob Firth, Laurie Smith, Midwestock/Patti McConville, Laurie Smith
Page 16: Envision, B.W. Hoffmann, Tony Stone Images/Paul Chesley, Leigh Beisch, Imagenes, Guy Kloppenburg
Page 40: Laurie Smith, Bob Firth, Midwestock/Ben Weddle, Imagenes/Kim Karpeles, Erik Rank
Page 72: Matthew Gilson, Bob Firth, Bob Firth, Laurie Smith, Per Breiehagen
Page 108: Laurie Smith, Erik Rank, Imagenes/Christopher Hirsheimer, Laurie Smith, Maria Stenzel

Time-Life Books is a division of Time Life Inc.

Time-Life is a trademark of Time Warner Inc.,

 and affiliated companies.

**TIME LIFE INC.**

President and CEO: **Jim Nelson**

**TIME-LIFE TRADE PUBLISHING**

Vice President and Publisher: **Neil Levin**

Vice President, Content Development:

 **Jennifer L. Pearce**

**WILLIAMS-SONOMA**

Founder and Vice-Chairman: **Chuck Williams**

Book Buyer: **Cecilia Michaelis**

**WELDON OWEN INC.**

Chief Executive Officer: **John Owen**

President: **Terry Newell**

Chief Operating Officer: **Larry Partington**

Vice President International Sales: **Stuart Laurence**

Associate Publisher: **Val Cipollone**

Editor: **Sarah Lemas**

Copy Editor: **Sharon Silva**

Consulting Editor: **Norman Kolpas**

Design: **Jane Palecek**

Production Manager: **Chris Hemesath**

Food Stylist: **George Dolese**

Prop Stylist: **Sara Slavin**

Studio Assistant: **Sheri Giblin**

Food Styling Assistant: **Leslie Busch**

Scenic Photo Research: **Caren Alpert**

The Williams-Sonoma New American Cooking Series
conceived and produced by Weldon Owen Inc.
814 Montgomery Street, San Francisco, CA 94133

In collaboration with Williams-Sonoma
3250 Van Ness Avenue, San Francisco, CA 94109

Separations by Bright Arts Graphics (S) Pte. Ltd.
Printed in Singapore by Tien Wah Press (Pte.) Ltd.

**A WELDON OWEN PRODUCTION**

Map copyright © Ann Field

First printed in 2001
10 9 8 7 6 5 4 3 2 1

Library of Congress
Cataloging-in-Publication Data

Dooley, Beth.
The heartland / general editor, Chuck Williams; recipes and
 text, Beth Dooley; photography, Leigh Beisch.
     p. cm. — (Williams-Sonoma New American Cooking)
   Includes index.
   ISBN 0-7370-2046-6
   1. Cookery, American--Midwestern style.  2. Middle
West—Social life and customs.  I. Williams, Chuck.
II. Title.  III. Series.
TX715.2.M53 D6596   2001
641.5977—dc21                    2001023701
                                       CIP

**A NOTE ON NUTRITIONAL ANALYSIS**
Each recipe is analyzed for significant nutrients per
serving. Not included in the analysis are ingredients
that are optional or added to taste, or are suggested
as an alternative or substitution either in the recipe
or in the recipe introduction. In recipes that yield
a range of servings, the analysis is for the middle
of that range.

**A NOTE ON WEIGHTS AND MEASURES**
All recipes include customary U.S. and metric
measurements. Metric conversions are based on
a standard developed for these books and have
been rounded off. Actual weights may vary.